THE PRIMARY TEACHER'S PET
Time-Savers for All Reasons and Seasons

S0-ACP-409

Written by Linda Schwartz
Illustrated by Beverly Armstrong

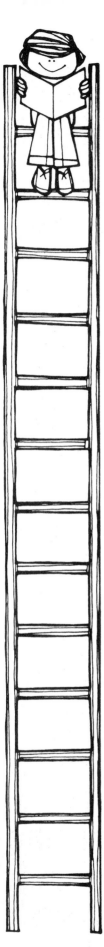

The Learning Works

Edited by Sherri M. Butterfield

The purchase of this book entitles the individual teacher to reproduce copies for use in the classroom.

The reproduction of any part for an entire school or school system or for commercial use is strictly prohibited.

No form of this work may be reproduced or transmitted or recorded without written permission from the publisher.

Copyright © 1984
THE LEARNING WORKS, INC.
P.O. Box 6187
Santa Barbara, CA 93160
All rights reserved.
Printed in the United States of America

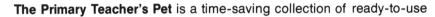

Introduction

The Primary Teacher's Pet is a time-saving collection of ready-to-use

- activities
- announcements
- awards
- birthday notes
- bookmarks
- borders
- calendars
- charts
- clip art
- contracts
- creative writing topics
- facts
- forms
- games
- get-well notes
- holiday suggestions
- independent study ideas
- invitations
- letters
- lists
- memos
- miscellaneous information
- name tags
- patterns
- rules
- tables
- word lists
- worksheets

Compiled by a former classroom teacher, these materials cover all major subject areas, including reading, phonics, language arts, math, social studies, and science, and are as up-to-date as computers. Many of them are all-purpose or open-ended and can be adapted easily to any event, occasion, or season. They have been selected for you, for your students, and for the aides, parents, substitutes, and others who work with you in educating children in the primary grades.

The pages in this book will help you get organized, get acquainted with your students, make assignments, keep track of student progress, give encouragement, recognize achievement, fill empty hours on rainy days, and communicate effectively with aides, substitute teachers, and parents—even when there isn't time! These pages will help students explore sounds and words, increase their vocabularies, practice math skills, keep track of assignments, make contracts governing work and behavior, and budget time.

But teaching and learning should not be all forms and facts. There's got to be some fun. Border patterns will help you decorate bulletin boards and walls. Clip art cutouts will make it easy for you to add a touch of whimsy to the tests and worksheets you create and to the announcements and letters you send home.

The Primary Teacher's Pet doesn't teach. Only you can do that. But its pages are packed with possibilities—ways to make teaching easier for you and learning more fun for your students. It's all of the many facts, forms, and ideas you need in one single, convenient package.

Contents

Contents
(continued)

Contents
(continued)

Forms and Notes

The Primary Teacher's Pet
©1984 — The Learning Works, Inc.

Birthday Scoops

Write each child's name, birthdate, and age in the appropriate place. Then keep this sheet for reference.

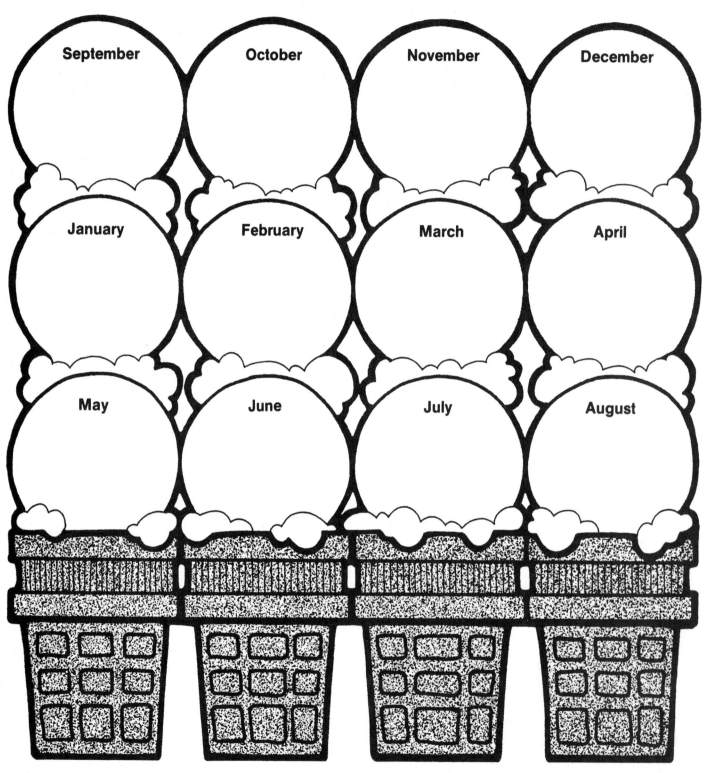

All-Purpose Chart

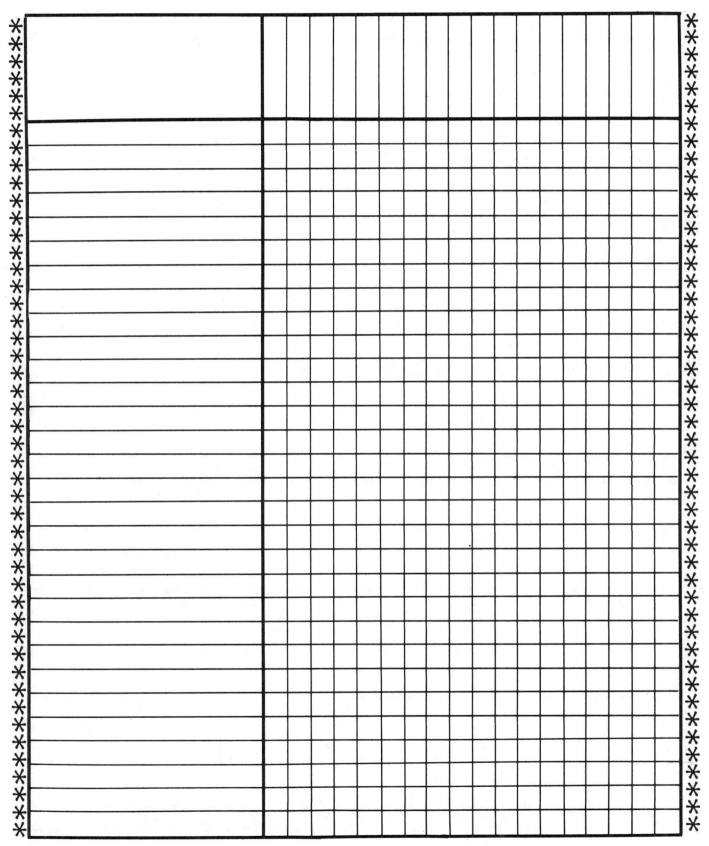

Any Month Calendar

SUNDAY	MONDAY	TUESDAY	WEDNESDAY	THURSDAY	FRIDAY	SATURDAY

Check when done.	# Things to Do Today
☐	_____
☐	_____
☐	_____
☐	_____
☐	_____
☐	_____
☐	_____
☐	_____
☐	_____
☐	_____
☐	_____
☐	_____

Handy Home Information

Name	Address	Telephone

A Call for Supplies

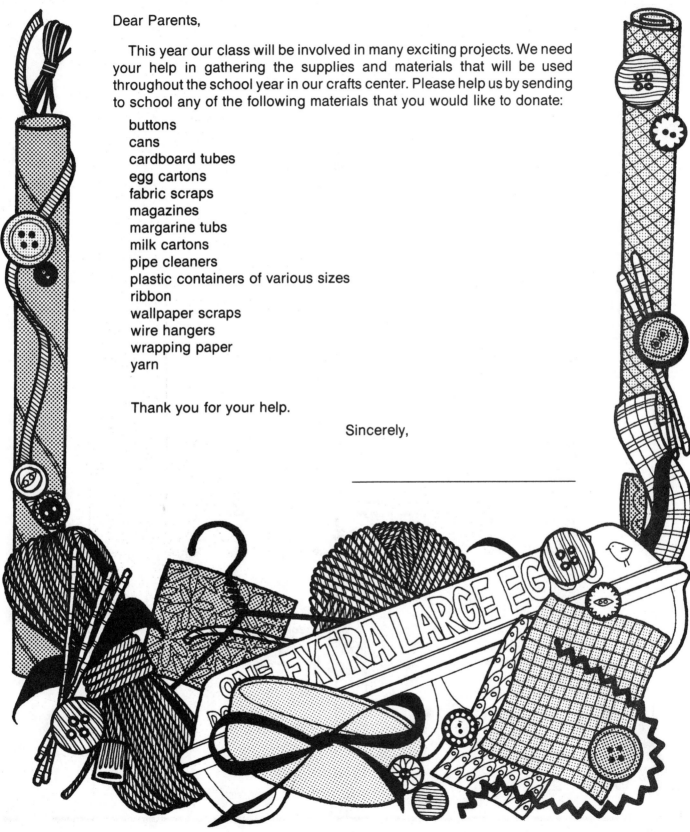

Dear Parents,

This year our class will be involved in many exciting projects. We need your help in gathering the supplies and materials that will be used throughout the school year in our crafts center. Please help us by sending to school any of the following materials that you would like to donate:

buttons
cans
cardboard tubes
egg cartons
fabric scraps
magazines
margarine tubs
milk cartons
pipe cleaners
plastic containers of various sizes
ribbon
wallpaper scraps
wire hangers
wrapping paper
yarn

Thank you for your help.

Sincerely,

_____

Portrait of Our Day

Dear Parents,

We hope you will come to see our classroom. Here's a copy of our daily schedule to help you plan your visit.

Sincerely,

_____

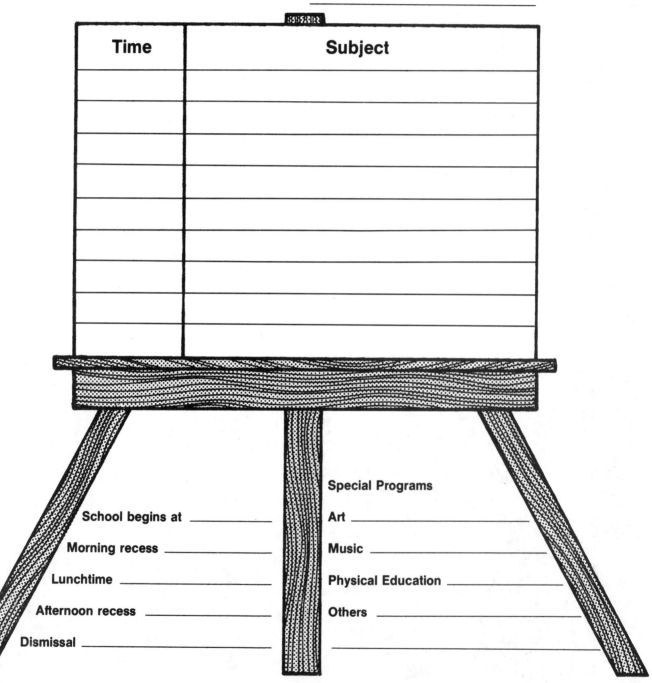

Time	Subject

School begins at _____

Morning recess _____

Lunchtime _____

Afternoon recess _____

Dismissal _____

Special Programs

Art _____

Music _____

Physical Education _____

Others _____

_____

Supply Checklist

Dear Parents,

Your child needs the supplies checked below for projects we will be doing in class.

- ☐ box for supplies
- ☐ pen
- ☐ pencils
- ☐ erasers
- ☐ ruler
- ☐ paste or white school glue
- ☐ crayons
- ☐ felt-tipped marking pens in assorted colors
- ☐ watercolors
- ☐ paintbrushes
- ☐ three-ring binder
- ☐ notebook paper
- ☐ construction paper in the following colors:

_____   _____

_____   _____

_____   _____

- ☐ old shirt to be used as an artist's smock

Please put your child's name on each item. A reminder will be sent home when our classroom supplies need to be replenished.

Thank you for your cooperation.

Sincerely,

_____

All About Assignments

Dear Parents,

Communication between home and school is vital to your child's success in the classroom.

To keep you informed and aware of what we are doing, I plan to send home a folder with papers and tests your child has completed in all areas of the curriculum every _____ .

Please take time to review and discuss these papers with your child. Then date and sign the form on your child's folder, keep the papers (unless otherwise noted), and have your child return the empty folder to me within two days.

Your cooperation is greatly appreciated.

Sincerely,

_____

Assignments

Dear Parents,

Inside this folder/envelope are _____ papers for the week. Please take time to review and discuss them with your child. Then date and sign this form and have your child return the empty folder to me by _____ of each week.

Date	Parent's Signature	Parent's Comments

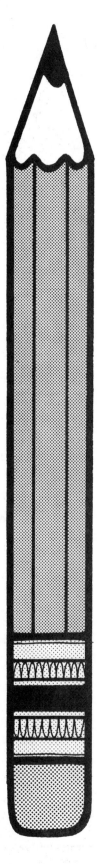

Help Wanted

Dear Parents,

We will be involved in a variety of projects during this school year and would appreciate your help. Please take time to fill out the attached form and have your child return it to me as soon as possible.

Sincerely,

_____

Name _____

Address _____

Phone _____

1. I am willing to help in the following areas:

☐ room mother	☐ dancing
☐ assistant room mother	☐ arts and crafts
☐ phone committee	☐ physical education
☐ sewing	☐ field trips
☐ cooking	☐ _____
☐ carpentry	☐ _____
☐ drama	☐ _____
☐ music	☐ _____

2. I would enjoy

☐ working with individual students	☐ making games
☐ working with small groups	☐ typing
☐ duplicating worksheets	☐ performing other clerical tasks
☐ grading papers	☐ _____
☐ preparing learning centers	☐ _____

3. I have the following special interest, talent, hobby, or occupation I would be willing to share with the class:

_____

4. The best time for me to help in the class is on

☐ Monday ☐ Tuesday ☐ Wednesday ☐ Thursday ☐ Friday

at _____ o'clock.

Our Class Newsletter

Date: _____ Room Number: _____ Issue Number: _____

Reading

Suggestions for Parents

Math

A Classroom Original

Name _____

Reading's a-Popping
My Work for the Week

Home Reading Record

Name _____

Date Started	Title	Author	Number of Pages	Date Finished

Homework Reminders

Reading

_____
_____
_____
_____
_____
_____

Science/ Social Studies

_____
_____
_____
_____
_____
_____

Math

_____
_____
_____
_____
_____
_____

Homework Reminder

_____
_____
_____
_____
_____
_____

Make-up Memo

To: _____

From: _____ Date: _____

Welcome back! While you were absent on _____,
you missed the following work:

Reading _____

_____

Math _____

_____

Spelling _____

_____

Social Studies/Science _____

_____

_____

Other _____

_____

_____

Please do this work and turn it in to me on or before _____ .

Contract

I, _____ ,
(Print your name on this line.)

plan to finish _____

_____

_____

on or before _____ .
(day or date)

Signed _____

_____   _____
(teacher's signature)   (date)

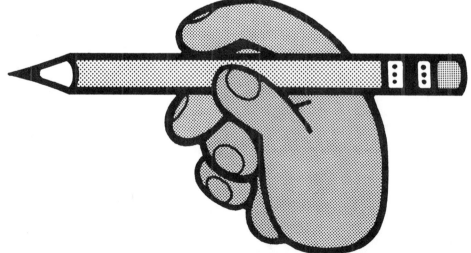

The Primary Teacher's Pet
©1984 — The Learning Works, Inc.

Behavior Contract

I, _____,
(Print your name on this line.)

will try my best to

☐ get to school on time.

☐ listen better in class.

☐ work harder.

☐ be neater in my work.

☐ turn in my work on time.

☐ be kinder to others.

☐ make better use of my time.

☐ keep my desk neat.

Signed _____
(Sign your name on this line.)

_____   _____
(teacher's signature)   (date)

☆ ☆ ☆ ☆ ☆ ☆ ☆ ☆ ☆ ☆

The Primary Teacher's Pet
©1984 — The Learning Works, Inc.

Name _____

Field Trip Fun

Date _____

Place I visited _____

Great Things I Saw	New Words I Learned
_____	_____
_____	_____
_____	_____
_____	_____

My favorite part of the trip was _____

_____

_____

On the back of this paper,
draw a picture to help you remember your trip.

Test-Taking Tips

General

1. Be ready to do your best. Review information that will be covered on the test. Get plenty of sleep on the night before the test. Eat a good breakfast on the morning of the test.
2. Pay close attention to the oral instructions.
3. Read the written instructions carefully.
4. Ask questions if you do not understand any of the instructions.
5. Know how much time you have, and use it wisely.
6. If you finish a section before time is up, look back over your work and check your answers.

Standardized Tests

1. Don't sharpen your pencil to a fine point. You can fill in the answer slots, circles, or boxes more easily with a blunt pencil.
2. First, answer the questions you feel sure about. Then, go back to the questions you are unsure of and need to think about.
3. Answer every question. Most standardized tests are scored on the basis of the total number of right answers, so it's a good idea to guess when you don't know.
4. Before you mark the answer sheet, check the question number against the answer number. That way you won't mark a *right* answer in the *wrong* place.

True-and-False Tests

1. Read each statement carefully. Sometimes a single word can trick you into giving the wrong answer.
2. When you see such words as **never**, **all**, and **always**, the statement is usually false.
3. In two-part statements, read each part carefully. If one part is true but the other part is false, the entire statement is false.

🍀 Helpful Hints 🍀
For My Substitute

1. A teacher who can help you is _____ in room _____.

2. Dependable students who can help you are _____
_____.

3. Classroom aides or volunteers who are scheduled to come in today are

Name	Time	Assignment
_____	_____	_____
_____	_____	_____
_____	_____	_____

4. You will find the following essential items in the places indicated.

Grade book _____

Lesson plans _____

Seating chart _____

Teacher's manuals _____

5. My duty today is _____
   (job)
at _____ at _____.
   (place)   (time)

6. My usual roll-call procedure is _____
_____.

7. The following students will be leaving the classroom during the day to attend special classes or to keep scheduled appointments:

Name	Time	Class/Reason	Room
_____	_____	_____	_____
_____	_____	_____	_____
_____	_____	_____	_____
_____	_____	_____	_____

8. The students on medication are _____
_____.

9. Emergency procedures are as follows: _____
_____
_____

Class List
For My Substitute

Girls	Boys

Lesson Plans
For My Substitute

Daily Schedule

Class Begins	_____
Morning Recess	_____
Lunch	_____
Afternoon Recess	_____
Dismissal	_____

Date _____

Time	Subject	Description

Aide Assignment Sheet
Working with Students

Name _____   Date _____

Activity	Student(s) Involved	Comments
☐ Listen to oral reading		
☐ Record dictation		
☐ Review flash cards		
☐ Assist with the following learning center activity:		
☐ Assist the following reading, math, writing, or spelling group:		
☐ Other		

Aide Assignment Sheet

Clerical Duties

Name ______________________ Date ______________________

Activity	Special Instructions	Needed By
☐ Type ditto masters	☐ of pages ________ in ________ ☐ of the attached sheets	
☐ Make a thermofax master	☐ of pages ________ in ________ ☐ of the attached sheets	
☐ Alphabetize		
☐ File		
☐ Run copies of ______________	Number of copies needed ________ Print ☐ on one side ☐ on two sides	
☐ Grade the attached papers		
☐ Make the described game or activity		
☐ Cut paper	Type of paper ______________ Color(s) ______________ Number of sheets ______________ Dimensions ______________	
☐ Design a calendar for the month of ______________	Suggested picture or theme ______________ ______________ ______________	
☐ Design a bulletin board	Subject ______________ Theme ______________ Purpose ______________	

©1984 — The Learning Works, Inc.

Activity Evaluation Sheet
For Aides

Name _____ **Date** _____

Assignment _____

To help me evaluate the effectiveness of the activity you supervised, please fill out this sheet and return it to me.

1. I felt that the activity was

☐ very effective

☐ satisfactory

☐ ineffective because _____

_____

_____

2. The following students had difficulty with the activity:

_____

_____

3. The behavior of the following students was a problem:

_____

_____

4. If the activity is done again, I would suggest that the following changes be made:

_____

_____

_____

5. Additional comments or suggestions: _____

_____

_____

_____

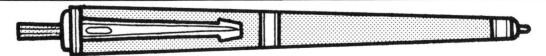

Aide Awards

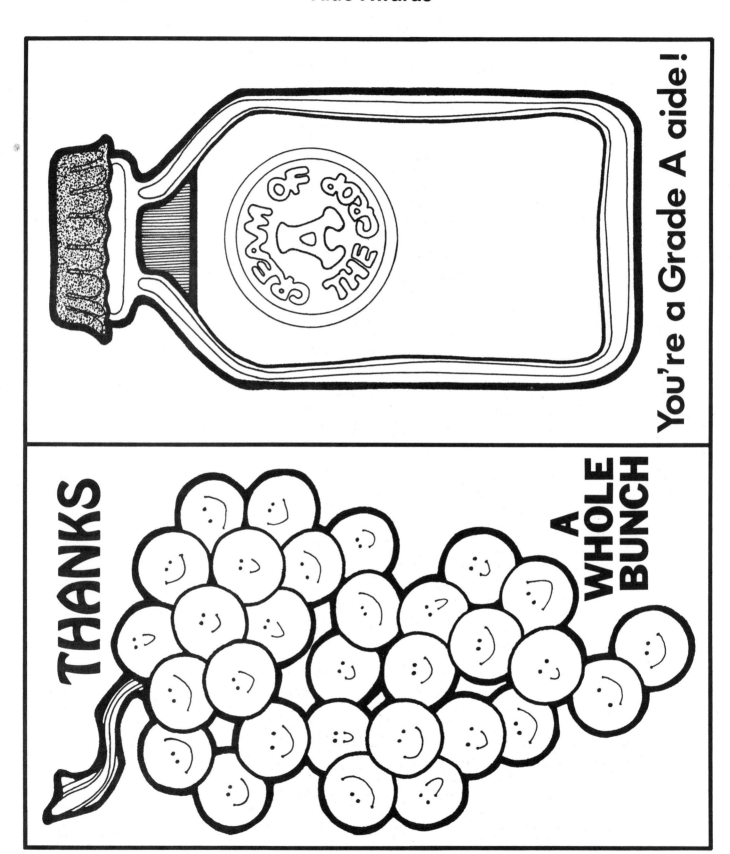

You're a Grade A aide!

THE GRADE OF A

THANKS

A WHOLE BUNCH

Name Tags

These all-purpose name tags are ideal for use by substitutes, visitors, and guest speakers and for use on field trips, at open house, and on many other occasions.

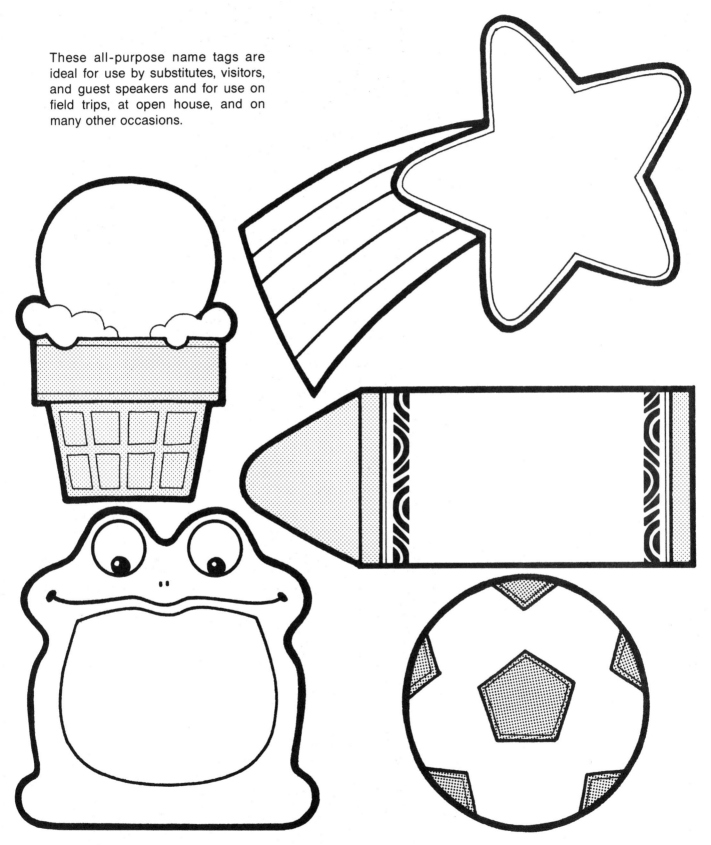

General Notes

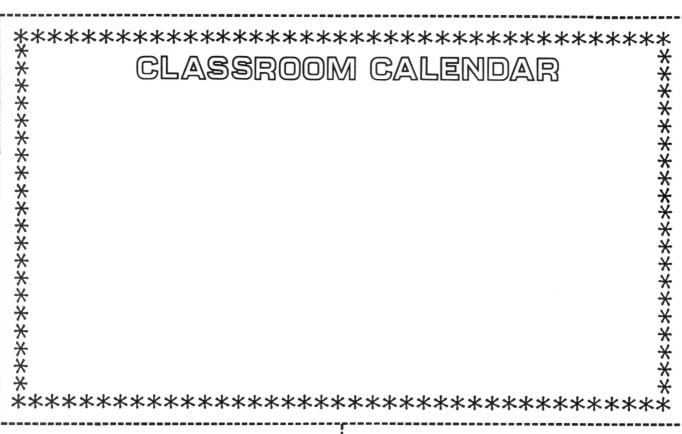

CLASSROOM CALENDAR

 TEACHER TALK

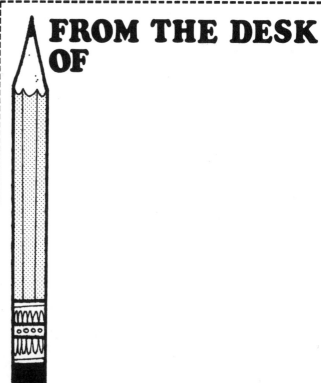

FROM THE DESK OF

Reminders

Announcements

Invitations

YOU'RE INVITED!

WE'LL BE LOOKING FOR YOU

Thank-You Notes

Get-Well Notes

WE MISS YOU! GET WELL SOON.

_____

PLEASE GET WELL SOON.

Happy Birthday Notes

Getting to Know You

How I See Me

Here is a picture of how I see myself on

_____ .
(date)

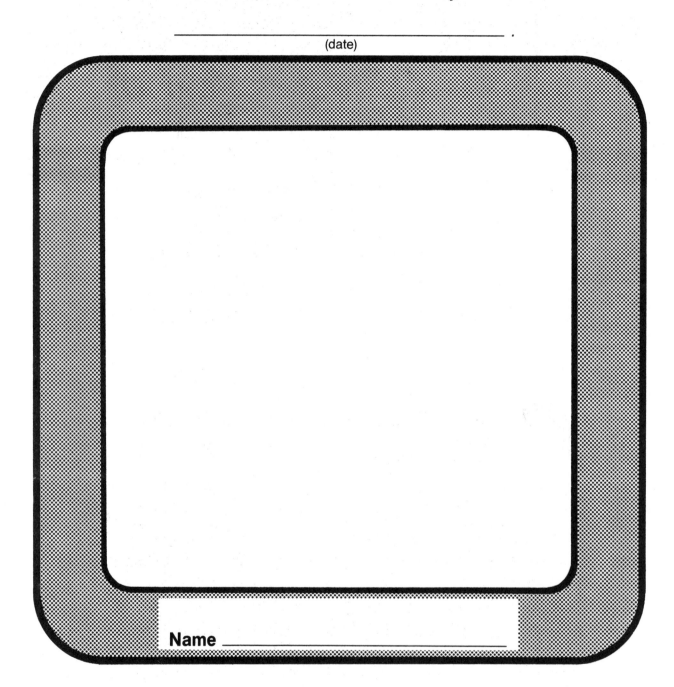

Name _____

Do this activity again later in the school year.
Compare your two pictures, and see how much you
have changed.

Who Are You?

My name is _____ .

Three things I like are

1. _____

2. _____

3. _____

Three things I dislike are

1. _____

2. _____

3. _____

I collect _____ .

Outside school, I take lessons in _____

_____ .

I think it would be fun to learn more about _____

_____ .

When I grow up, I want to be _____

_____ .

Name _____

My Favorites

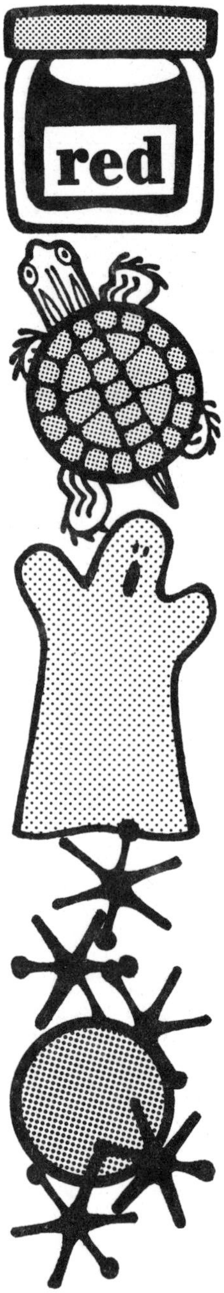

animal _____

book _____

color _____

day of the week _____

drink _____

food _____

hobby _____

holiday _____

movie _____

place to visit _____

song _____

sport or game _____

subject in school _____

television show _____

thing to wear _____

toy _____

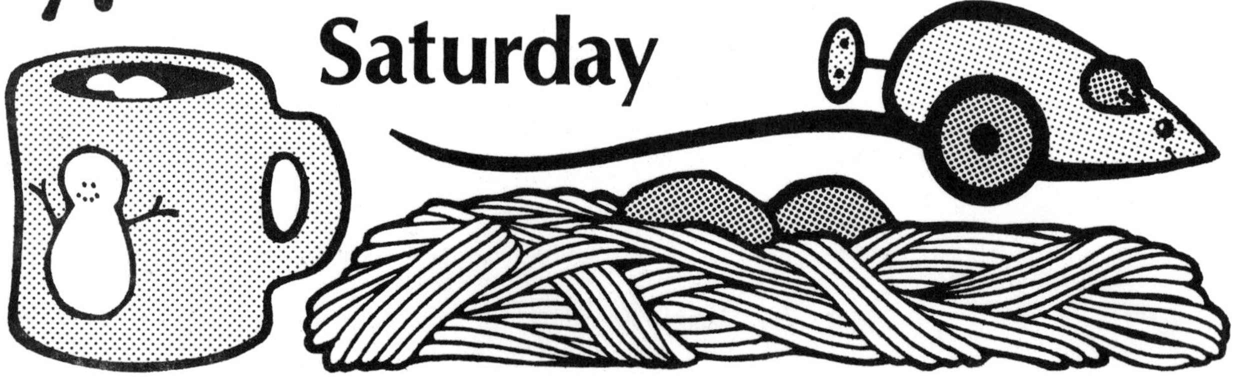

Saturday

Name _____

Things I Do

Put an **X** in the box beside each thing you do.

I like to
- [ ] build models
- [ ] camp
- [ ] climb trees
- [ ] do puzzles
- [ ] draw and color
- [ ] finger-paint
- [ ] fly kites
- [ ] go to the movies
- [ ] ice-skate
- [ ] jump rope
- [ ] listen to music
- [ ] paint
- [ ] read
- [ ] ride a bike
- [ ] roller skate
- [ ] sew
- [ ] ski
- [ ] swim
- [ ] watch television

I collect
- [ ] cards
- [ ] coins
- [ ] dolls
- [ ] rocks
- [ ] shells
- [ ] stamps

I play
- [ ] basketball
- [ ] cards
- [ ] checkers
- [ ] dolls
- [ ] dominoes
- [ ] football
- [ ] hide-and-seek
- [ ] marbles
- [ ] soccer
- [ ] softball
- [ ] tag

Name _____

The I-N-G Me

On each numbered line, write one word that
ends with the letters *i-n-g.*
In each box, draw a picture of you doing the
thing that word names.

eating

laughing

singing

1. _____

2. _____

3. _____

Name _____

My Family Banner

In space **1**, draw a picture of your family.

In space **2**, write your family's last name.

In space **3**, draw a picture of something you are good at.

In space **4**, draw a picture of your family doing something together.

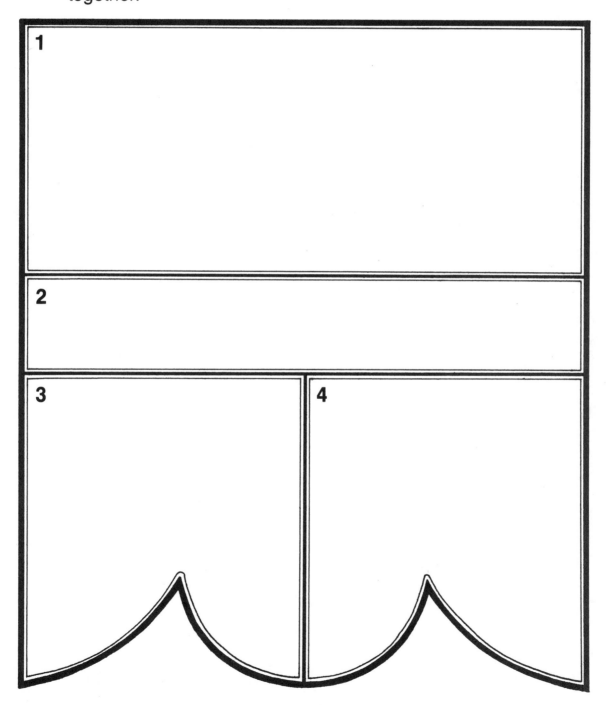

Name _____

In My Future

In space **1**, draw a picture of something you will be doing this summer.

In space **2**, draw a picture of a place you would like to visit someday.

In space **3**, draw a picture of the job you would like to have.

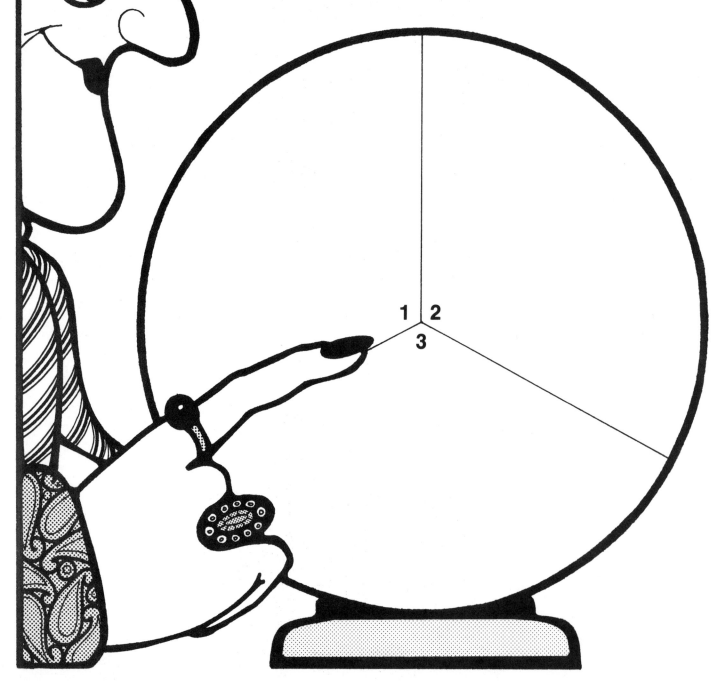

Reading and Language Arts

Rules for Dividing Words into Syllables

1. A syllable is a group of letters sounded together.

2. Each syllable must have at least one vowel sound.

3. A word cannot have more syllables than vowel sounds.

4. Words pronounced as one syllable should not be divided.

   arm   best   helped   through

5. A word containing two consonants between two vowels (**vccv**) is divided between the two consonants.

   vc cv   **vc cv**   **vc cv**   **vc cv**
   af-ter   bag-gage   pret-ty   sis-ter

6. In a two-syllable word containing a single consonant between two vowels (**vcv**), the consonant usually begins the second syllable.

   v cv   **v cv**   **v cv**   **v cv**
   be-gin   cra-zy   pi-rate   to-day

7. In a word ending in **-le**, the consonant in front of the **-le** usually begins the last syllable.

   can-<u>d</u>le   cir-<u>c</u>le   mar-<u>b</u>le   ta-<u>b</u>le

8. Compound words usually are divided between their word parts.

   after-noon   any-thing   rain-bow   sun-shine

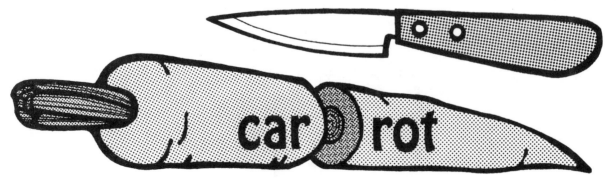

Rules for Accenting Syllables

1. In a two-syllable word containing a double consonant, the first syllable is usually accented.

   ap' ple   dad' dy   hap' py   rib' bon

2. In a two-syllable word where the second syllable has two or more vowels, the second syllable is usually accented.

   a-round'   be-lieve'   dis-ease'   ex-plain'

3. In words ending in **-ion**, **-tion**, **-sion**, **-ial**, and **-cial**, the syllable in front of these endings is usually accented.

   at-ten' tion   de-ci' sion   di-rec' tion   of-fi' cial

4. In a compound word made up of two one-syllable words, the first word is usually accented.

   base' ball   bed' room   card' board   high' way

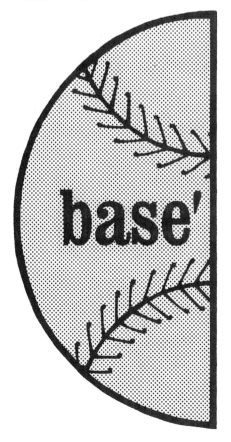

The Blend Friends

ch

chain	cheese
chair	chest
chalk	chew
champ	chick
chance	chief
change	chill
chant	chimp
chap	chin
charm	china
chart	chip
chase	chirp
chat	choke
cheap	choose
cheat	chop
check	chum
cheek	chunk
cheer	churn

dr

drab
drag
drain
drape
draw
dread
dream
dress
drift
drill
drink
drip
drive
droop
drop
drum
dry

gr

grab	greet
grace	grid
grade	grief
grain	grill
grand	grim
grant	grin
grape	grind
graph	grip
grass	grit
grate	groan
grave	groom
gray	ground
graze	group
grease	grow
great	growl
greed	gruff
green	grunt

sh

shack	shell
shade	shift
shake	shine
shall	ship
shame	shirt
shape	shop
share	shore
shark	short
shave	shot
shawl	should
she	shout
shed	shove
sheep	show
sheet	shut
shelf	shy

th

that	thing
thaw	think
the	third
their	thirty
them	this
then	those
there	though
these	thought
they	thud
thick	thumb
thin	thump

wh

whale	which
wharf	while
what	whine
wheat	whip
wheel	whirl
when	white
where	whiz
whether	why

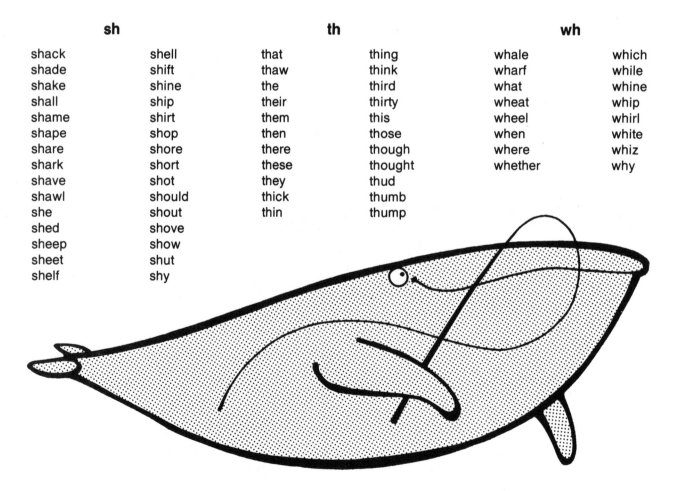

Rhyming Word Families

all	an	at	bag	bake
ball	ban	bat	gag	brake
call	bran	cat	hag	cake
fall	can	chat	jag	drake
gall	clan	fat	lag	fake
hall	fan	flat	nag	flake
mall	man	gnat	rag	lake
pall	pan	hat	sag	make
small	plan	mat	shag	quake
stall	ran	pat	tag	rake
tall	scan	rat		sake
wall	tan	sat		shake
	than	scat		snake
	van	slat		stake
		spat		take
		that		wake
		vat		

bank	bay	beat	bed	bend
blank	clay	cheat	bled	blend
crank	day	cleat	bred	end
drank	fray	eat	fed	fend
flank	gay	feat	fled	lend
frank	gray	heat	led	mend
hank	hay	meat	red	send
plank	jay	neat	shed	spend
rank	lay	pleat	shred	tend
sank	may	treat	sled	trend
spank	pay	wheat	sped	vend
tank	play		wed	
thank	pray			
yank	ray			
	say			
	stay			
	sway			
	tray			
	way			

The fat cat sat on the flat mat.

Rhyming Word Families
(continued)

best	bill	bin	bit	brick
chest	chill	din	fit	chick
jest	dill	fin	flit	flick
nest	drill	gin	grit	kick
pest	gill	kin	hit	lick
rest	hill	pin	it	nick
test	kill	sin	kit	pick
west	mill	skin	lit	sick
wrest	pill	thin	mitt	slick
zest	quill	tin	nit	stick
	skill	win	pit	tick
	spill		quit	trick
	still		sit	wick
	will		slit	
			spit	
			wit	

bright	bring	blot	blow	clear
flight	cling	clot	crow	dear
fright	ding	cot	flow	ear
knight	fling	dot	glow	fear
light	king	got	grow	gear
might	ring	hot	know	hear
night	sing	lot	low	rear
right	sling	not	mow	sear
sight	spring	plot	row	shear
slight	sting	pot	show	spear
tight	swing	rot	slow	tear
	thing	shot	snow	year
	wing	slot	sow	
	wring	spot	tow	
		tot		
		trot		

In the spring, the king liked to swing and sing.

Name _____

Mighty Manuscript

Aa Bb Cc Dd Ee
Ff Gg Hh Ii Jj Kk
Ll Mm Nn Oo Pp
Qq Rr Ss Tt Uu
Vv Ww Xx Yy Zz

Name _____

The Cursive Castle

Synonym Soda

Synonyms are words that mean the same thing.

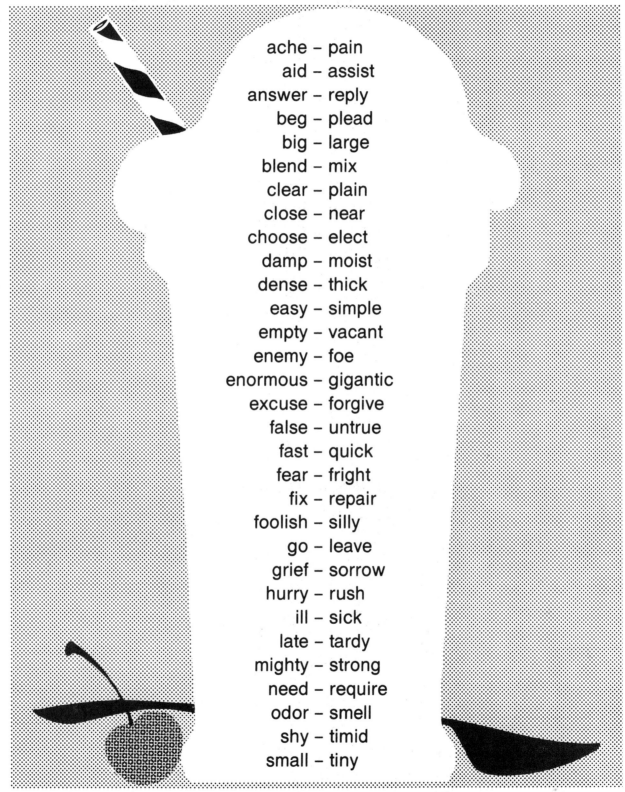

ache – pain
aid – assist
answer – reply
beg – plead
big – large
blend – mix
clear – plain
close – near
choose – elect
damp – moist
dense – thick
easy – simple
empty – vacant
enemy – foe
enormous – gigantic
excuse – forgive
false – untrue
fast – quick
fear – fright
fix – repair
foolish – silly
go – leave
grief – sorrow
hurry – rush
ill – sick
late – tardy
mighty – strong
need – require
odor – smell
shy – timid
small – tiny

Antonym Animals

Antonyms are words that mean opposite things.
They are sometimes called **opposites**.

above – below	dry – wet	high – low
alike – different	dull – shiny	in – out
always – never	early – late	joy – sorrow
asleep – awake	easy – hard	left – right
back – front	empty – full	lose – win
bad – good	fancy – plain	narrow – wide
begin – end	far – near	new – old
best – worst	fast – slow	no – yes
big – little	fat – thin	off – on
bottom – top	few – many	often – seldom
clean – dirty	first – last	part – whole
close – open	foolish – wise	poor – rich
cold – hot	fresh – stale	pretty – ugly
crooked – straight	go – stop	right – wrong
dark – light	happy – sad	short – tall
day – night	hard – soft	start – stop
deep – shallow	healthy – sick	strong – weak
down – up	heavy – light	tender – tough

Hooray for Homonyms

Homonyms are words that sound the same but are spelled in different ways and mean different things.

ad – add	gait – gate	pail – pale
ant – aunt	grate – great	pain – pane
ate – eight	hair – hare	pair – pear
ball – bawl	hall – haul	peace – piece
bare – bear	hay – hey	peak – peek
be – bee	hear – here	plain – plane
beat – beet	heard – herd	read – red
been – bin	hoarse – horse	real – reel
blew – blue	hole – whole	right – write
board – bored	hour – our	road – rode
buy – by	in – inn	rose – rows
cell – sell	knead – need	sail – sale
cent – sent	knew – new	sea – see
creak – creek	knight – night	son – sun
dear – deer	knot – not	tail – tale
do – due	know – no	their – there
eye – I	made – maid	threw – through
fir – fur	mail – male	toe – tow
flour – flower	meat – meet	waist – waste
foul – fowl	one – won	war – wore

Period .

Put a **period** at the end of a sentence
that is a statement or a command.

Take me to your leader.

Put a **period** after an abbreviation,
the shortened form of a word.

Mr. Fred Frimple saw something strange on St. James Street.

Put a **period** after an initial,
or single letter
used in place of a name.

I. M. Strange is a creature from Mars.

Comma ,

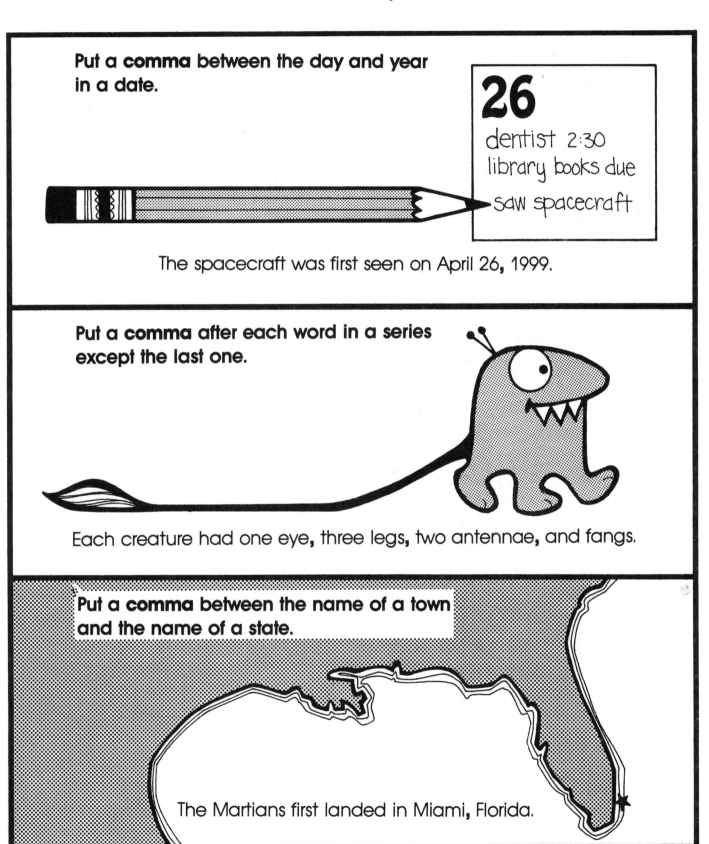

Put a **comma** between the day and year in a date.

26
dentist 2:30
library books due
saw spacecraft

The spacecraft was first seen on April 26, 1999.

Put a **comma** after each word in a series except the last one.

Each creature had one eye, three legs, two antennae, and fangs.

Put a **comma** between the name of a town and the name of a state.

The Martians first landed in Miami, Florida.

Comma ,
(continued)

**Put a comma after the word yes or no
at the beginning of a sentence.**

Yes, I was really frightened when I saw the creature.

**Put a comma after the greeting in a personal letter
and after the closing in all letters.**

Dear Joe,
    You will never guess what
happened! Creatures from Mars
were discovered here today.
                  Your pal,
                  Mike

Other Punctuation Marks

Question Mark **?**

**Put a question mark at the end of a sentence
that asks a question.**

Have you ever seen a creature from Mars**?**

Exclamation Point **!**

**Put an exclamation point at the end of a sentence
that shows strong feeling.**

The Martians have landed**!**

" Quotation Marks **"**

**Put quotation marks around words that someone says.
Put one set of marks before the talking starts.
Put the other set after the period, question mark, or exclamation point
to show that the talking has stopped.**

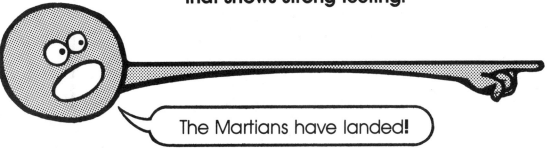

Steve said, **"**The spacecraft flew over my house!**"**

Parts of Speech

Part of Speech	Definition	Examples
noun	A **noun** is the name of a person, place, thing, or idea.	girl city dress happiness
verb	A **verb** expresses action or being.	sing is
adjective	An **adjective** describes a noun or pronoun by telling how many, what kind, or which one.	five, few pretty, empty that, this
adverb	An **adverb** describes a verb, adjective, or another adverb by telling how, when, or where.	slowly now there
pronoun	A **pronoun** is used in place of a noun.	I, you, we he, she, they someone

slowly

Rules for Forming Plurals

1. Most words are made plural by adding the letter **s** to the singular form.

    cat   cats
    desk   desks

2. Words ending in **ch**, **s**, **sh**, **x**, and **z** are made plural by adding the letters **es** to the singular form.

    box   boxes
    inch   inches

3. Most words ending in **a vowel and y** are made plural by adding the letter **s**.

    boy   boys
    monkey   monkeys

4. Words ending in **a consonant and y** are made plural by changing the **y** to **i** and adding **es**.

    bunny   bunnies
    penny   pennies

5. Most words ending in **f** or **fe** are made plural by changing the **f** or **fe** to **v** and adding **es**.

    knife   knives
    thief   thieves

6. Some words ending in **f** are made plural by simply adding **s**.

    chief   chiefs
    roof   roofs

7. Some words do not follow any of these rules. They have unusual plural forms.

    deer   deer
    ox   oxen
    tooth   teeth

Compound Party

airline	doorbell
airmail	doormat
airplane	downtown
airport	drawback
backbone	drumstick
backfire	dugout
background	eardrum
bareback	everyone
barefoot	everything
barnyard	eyebrow
baseball	eyelash
basketball	farmhouse
birthday	fingernail
blackberry	fingerprint
blackboard	fireplace
blindfold	fireworks
bluebird	football
breakfast	forever
bulldog	frostbite
butterfly	fullback
campfire	glassware
classroom	goldfish
cupcake	grapefruit
daytime	grapevine

Compound Party
(continued)

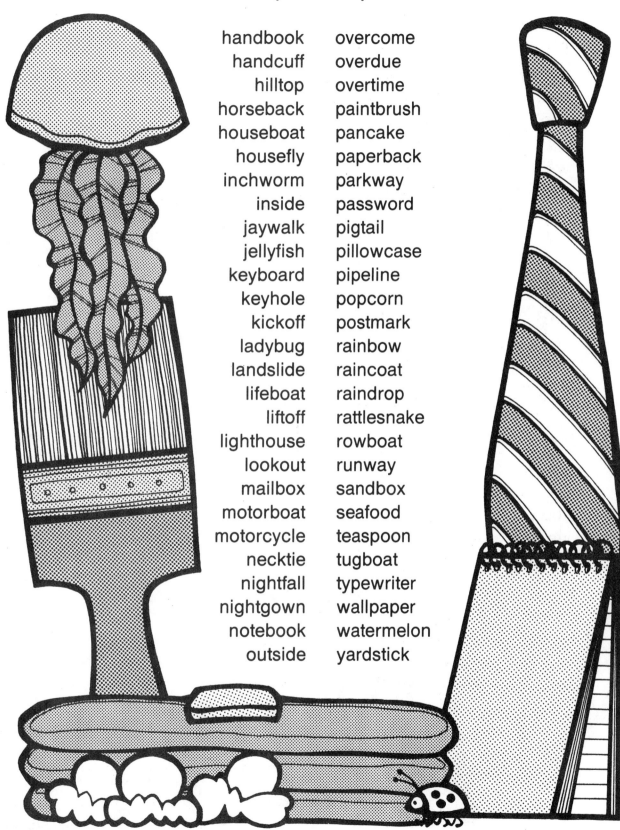

handbook	overcome
handcuff	overdue
hilltop	overtime
horseback	paintbrush
houseboat	pancake
housefly	paperback
inchworm	parkway
inside	password
jaywalk	pigtail
jellyfish	pillowcase
keyboard	pipeline
keyhole	popcorn
kickoff	postmark
ladybug	rainbow
landslide	raincoat
lifeboat	raindrop
liftoff	rattlesnake
lighthouse	rowboat
lookout	runway
mailbox	sandbox
motorboat	seafood
motorcycle	teaspoon
necktie	tugboat
nightfall	typewriter
nightgown	wallpaper
notebook	watermelon
outside	yardstick

Contraction Critter

Be

I'm	I am
you're	you are
he's	he is
she's	she is
it's	it is
we're	we are
they're	they are

Not

isn't	is not
aren't	are not
won't	will not
can't	cannot
don't	do not
hasn't	has not
haven't	have not

Would

I'd	I would
you'd	you would
he'd	he would
she'd	she would
we'd	we would
they'd	they would
who'd	who would

Will

I'll	I will
you'll	you will
he'll	he will
she'll	she will
it'll	it will
we'll	we will
they'll	they will
who'll	who will

Have

I've	I have
you've	you have
we've	we have
they've	they have

Word of the Week

Ideas for Using the Word of the Week. The words listed on pages 71-75 are common words that are uncommon in the working vocabularies of primary-aged children. Select and feature one or more of these words each week. Write them on the board, and encourage students to discover their pronunciations and meanings, and then to use them in oral and written communication. Periodically add these words to spelling lists as bonus words, use them as a special challenge for good spellers, or reward children for finding them in magazines and newspapers or for hearing them in everyday conversation.

absent (ab'-sənt) *adj.*—not present; missing; away: *She was **absent** from school because she was sick.*

ancient (ān'-shənt) *adj.*—very old: *We saw an **ancient** vase in the museum.*

bawl (bôl) *verb*—to shout or cry loudly: *I heard the baby **bawl** after she fell and bumped her head.*

blend (blend) *verb*—to mix together completely: *The cook had to **blend** the eggs and milk to make the cake batter.*

clever (klev'-ər) *adj.*—quick in learning; showing skill: *The magician did a **clever** trick with cards.*

cling (kling) *verb*—to hold fast or stick closely: *Cockleburs **cling** to your socks after you walk through tall grass.*

dim (dim) *adj.*—not bright or clear: *He could not see well enough to read because the light was so **dim**.*

drowsy (drou'-zē) *adj.*—sleepy; ready to fall asleep: *The child was **drowsy** after a day at the beach.*

eel (ēl) *noun*—a long, slippery fish that looks like a snake: *We saw an **eel** in the ocean.*

enormous (i-nôr'-məs) *adj.*—very large; huge: *The dinosaur was **enormous** and had to move slowly.*

Word of the Week
(continued)

feeble (fē′-bəl) *adj.*—weak; not strong: *The **feeble** old woman had to walk very slowly.*

flair (flaər) *noun*—a natural ability; talent: *Bev has a **flair** for drawing and painting.*

gadget (gaj′-ət) *noun*—a small tool; an interesting, unfamiliar, or unusual device: *When dad could not open the jar lid with his hands, he used a **gadget** to pry it off.*

glimpse (glimps) *noun*—a quick look; a glance: *She caught a **glimpse** of her friend in the crowd at the parade.*

hibernate (hī′-bər-nāt) *verb*—to spend the winter sleeping: *Many bears **hibernate** in caves.*

hoist (hoist) *verb*—to lift, boost, or pull up: *It took three men to **hoist** the heavy piano when we moved into our new house.*

invisible (in-viz′-ə-bəl) *adj.*—not able to be seen; not visible; hidden: *You know that the wind is there even though it is **invisible**.*

island (ī′-lənd) *noun*—an area of land that is completely surrounded by water and is smaller than a continent: *The crew from the wrecked ship rowed toward the **island**.*

jab (jab) *verb*—to poke with something sharp or pointed: *Be careful not to **jab** yourself with that stick.*

jerk (jurk) *noun*—a sudden, sharp pull or twist: *The elevator started up with a **jerk**.*

Word of the Week
(continued)

katydid (kā'-tē-did) *noun*—a large, green grasshopper: *The cat chased the* **katydid** *on our lawn.*

knead (nēd) *verb*—to work and press with the hands: *I helped mom* **knead** *the dough when we baked bread together.*

ledge (lej) *noun*—a narrow shelf; a ridge of rock: *I put my shell collection on the window* **ledge** *in my room.*

loyal (loi'-əl) *adj.*—faithful and true: *Sarah is a* **loyal** *friend.*

muggy (mug'-ē) *adj.*—warm and damp: *It was a* **muggy**, *uncomfortable day.*

munch (munch) *verb*—to chew in a noisy way: *My rabbit likes to* **munch** *on carrots.*

neglect (ni-glekt') *verb*—to give little attention, care, or respect to: *Do not* **neglect** *your teeth.*

numb (num) *adj.*—having lost feeling or movement: *My fingers quickly grew* **numb** *in the cold night air.*

odor (ō'-dər) *noun*—smell; scent: *I love the* **odor** *of bread baking in the oven.*

otter (ot'-ər) *noun*—a fish-eating, web-footed water animal that looks like a weasel and is valued for its thick, dark brown fur: *We fed the* **otter** *a fish at the zoo.*

prank (prangk) *noun*—a playful trick or joke: *On April Fools' Day, my brother played a* **prank** *on me.*

puncture (pungh'-chər) *verb*—to make a hole in something with a sharp object: *It is easy to* **puncture** *a balloon.*

Word of the Week
(continued)

quit (kwit) *verb*—to stop or leave: *I do not want to **quit** taking dance lessons.*

quiver (kwiv′-ər) *verb*—to shake slightly; shiver: *The leaves **quiver** in the breeze.*

rapid (rap′-id) *adj.*—very fast: *The runner moved at a **rapid** pace.*

relic (rel′-ik) *noun*—a thing left from the past: *The vase is a **relic** from grandmother's day.*

scarce (skers) *adj.*—difficult to get or find: *Rain is **scarce** in the Mojave Desert.*

snug (snug) *adj.*—fitting closely; comfortable and warm; cozy: *On a cold, rainy night, it's nice to get into my **snug** bed.*

tattle (tat′-əl) *verb*—to tell tales or secrets: *When I do something wrong, my little brother likes to **tattle** on me.*

timid (tim′-id) *adj.*—shy; easily frightened: *The deer is a **timid** animal.*

unite (yū-nīt′) *verb*—to bring or join together; to make one; combine: *Players **unite** to form a team.*

unusual (un-yū′-zhū-əl) *adj.*—not common or usual: *It is **unusual** to find water in the desert.*

Word of the Week
(continued)

vague (vāg) *adj.*—not clear or definite: *I got lost because his directions were **vague**.*

vanish (van'-ish) *verb*—to go out of sight; disappear: *I saw the plane **vanish** in the clouds.*

wilt (wilt) *verb*—to droop or fade; to become limp: *Flowers **wilt** in the hot sun.*

witty (wit'-ē) *adj.*—amusing in a clever way: *The comedian told a **witty** joke.*

xylem (zī'-ləm) *noun*—the woody part of plants found in the stalk or stem: *The **xylem** carries water from the roots of a plant up to its leaves.*

xylophone (zī'-lə-fōn) *noun*—a musical instrument made up of rows of wooden or metal bars of different lengths: *She used two wooden hammers to strike the keys of the **xylophone**.*

yearly (yēr'-lē) *adj.*—happening once a year: *During the summer, we made our **yearly** trip to the cabin.*

yowl (youl) *noun*—a long, loud wailing sound: *The **yowl** of the wolf could be heard from far away.*

zip (zip) *verb*—to fasten or close with a zipper: *She had to **zip** her jacket before going outside.*

zoom (zūm) *verb*—to move suddenly upward or climb quickly: *When the pilot saw the mountain, he made the airplane **zoom** so that it would not hit the peak.*

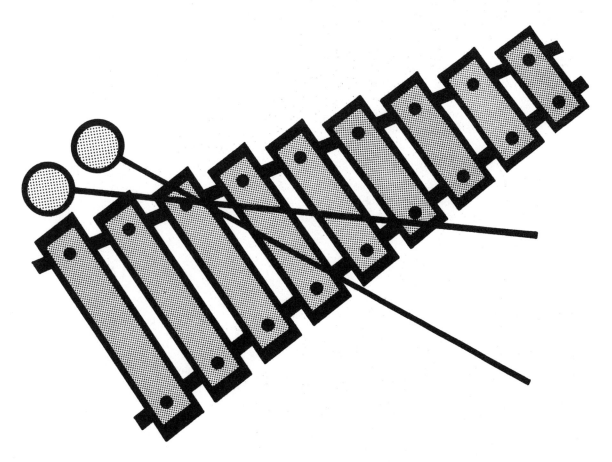

Great Ideas
For Using the Creative Writing Topics
Listed on Pages 77-81

Theme of the Week

Pick one of the topics, such as Animal Stories, as a theme for the week. Reproduce the list of suggested topics and post it at a creative writing center. Ask each student to choose a topic and to develop a short story based on that topic. Display completed stories on a bulletin board. Change the theme on a weekly or monthly basis.

Go Fish

Reproduce the list of suggested topics and cut the topics apart. Place them in a fish bowl, can, or box. Encourage students to "fish" for topics.

Howdy Partner

Have students work in pairs and collaborate on a story based on a selected topic.

Monthly Magazine

Start a monthly magazine featuring outstanding stories written from the suggested topics. Have students illustrate their stories. Share copies of the magazine in class and send them home for parents to enjoy.

Tape a Tale

Using a group of about six to eight students, select one topic. While you tape record, have one student begin a story based on the selected topic. When you give a signal, the next student continues the story, keeping the same main character and following the same story line until the signal is given again. Continue in this manner until each student has added to the story. Replay the tape for fun—and for other members of the class.

Spin a Story

Place one of the topic lists at a creative writing center. Make a wheel with a spinner as shown, numbering from one through twelve. Have students spin the spinner and write a story using the topic to which the arrow points.

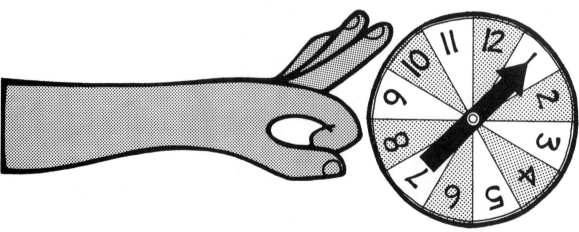

Creative Writing Topics
Animal Stories

1. Puppy Power

2. A Turtle in Trouble

3. The Baboon That Loved Bubble Gum

4. The Empty Cage

5. Pet Problems

6. The Burglar and the Bear

7. The Pet Store Window

8. A Skunk in the Trunk

9. The Laughing Lion

10. One Puppy Too Many

11. Horace, the Roller-Skating Hippo

12. The Cat in the Candy Store

Creative Writing Topics
Just for Fun

1. Giggling Gus

2. The Magical Mirror

3. Mummy on the Loose

4. When Numbers Disappeared

5. The Tri-Eyed Slitherwart

6. The Secret Formula of Dr. Ficklepickle

7. The Purple House on Murple Street

8. Miss Mandy and the Candy Machine

9. A Cow on the Roof

10. The Surprise Package

11. The Chocolate Chip Gang

12. The Kid with the Green Face

Creative Writing Topics
Mystery

1. The Fortune Cookie Caper

2. Super Spy for the FBI

3. A Scream in the Night

4. The Creature of Willow Creek

5. Up from the Deep

6. The Disappearing Ghost

7. The Phone Booth Mystery

8. The Empty Room

9. Swamp Creature

10. The Monster That Took over the Earth

11. The Nightmare

12. The Cave of the Dragon

Creative Writing Topics
Sports

1. My Turn at Bat

2. Tops on the Team

3. How I Saved the Game

4. Slugger Strikes Out

5. The Winning Goal

6. Super Stars

7. Bessie of Baseball Fame

8. The Swim Win

9. On the Run

10. The Champ

11. The Soccer Star

12. New to the Team

Creative Writing Topics
General

1. Decisions, Decisions

2. Lost at Sea

3. A Special Secret

4. Wally, the Wizard

5. A Kid in Trouble

6. The Spider That Grew and Grew

7. A Narrow Escape

8. Without a Warning

9. On the Island of Goochie-Geechie

10. Trapped!

11. A Skunk in My Tub

12. Was I Ever Mad!

Name _____

Picture This

On the line, write the name of the story or book you read.
On the TV screen, draw and color a picture of something that happened in your story.
Show your picture to the class, and tell what you liked best about the story.

Name of My Book

_____

The Book Beast

Use this beast to tell others about a book you enjoyed. Fill it out. Then cut it out, and put it on the board.

My name is

The name of my book is

It was written by

On the lines below, write about the part of the book that you liked best.

Bookmarks

The Parts of a Book

title page   the second printed page in a book and the page on which the title of the book, the name of the author, the name of the illustrator, and the name of the publisher are listed

> **title**   the name of a story or book
> **author**   the person who wrote the book
> **illustrator** the person who drew the pictures
> **publisher**   the company that printed the book

copyright page   usually the back of the title page, this page includes the copyright notice, the name of the person or company holding the copyright, and the year in which the book was copyrighted

dedication page   page that carries a brief statement in which the author inscribes or addresses his or her book to someone as a way of thanking or complimenting that person

table of contents   a list of the main parts of a book by title and page number in the order in which they appear

body or text   the main part of a book

glossary   an alphabetical list of the hard or unusual words used in a book with their meanings and pronunciations

bibliography   a list of the articles and the other books referred to in a book or used by the author in writing it

index   an alphabetical list of the names or topics covered in a book, together with the numbers of the pages on which they are defined, explained, or discussed

Name _____

The Book Clown

Fill in the missing words.
Use the words in the balloons to help you.
Color the balloons as you use the words in them.

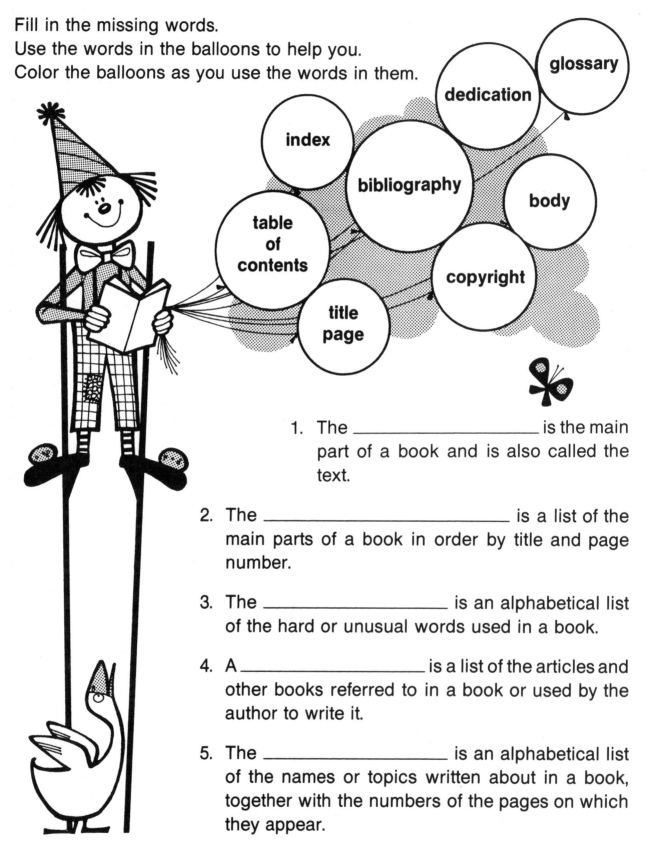

1. The _____ is the main part of a book and is also called the text.

2. The _____ is a list of the main parts of a book in order by title and page number.

3. The _____ is an alphabetical list of the hard or unusual words used in a book.

4. A _____ is a list of the articles and other books referred to in a book or used by the author to write it.

5. The _____ is an alphabetical list of the names or topics written about in a book, together with the numbers of the pages on which they appear.

Name _____

New Words I Know

Here are some new words that I found while reading.

Word	Meaning

Name _____

Pickled Plurals

Write the plural of each word.

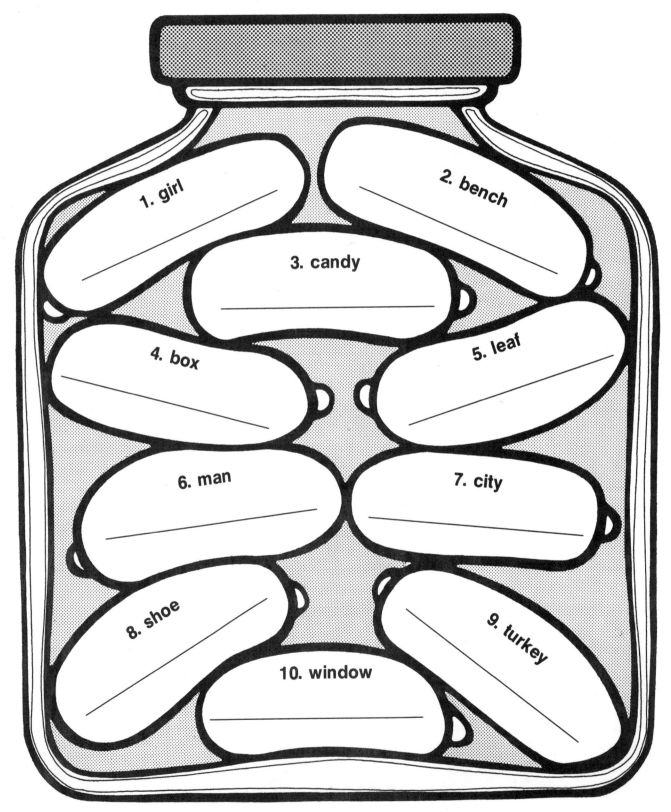

1. girl _____

2. bench _____

3. candy _____

4. box _____

5. leaf _____

6. man _____

7. city _____

8. shoe _____

9. turkey _____

10. window _____

Name _____

Alphabet Animals

Write the names of these animals in alphabetical order on the lines below.

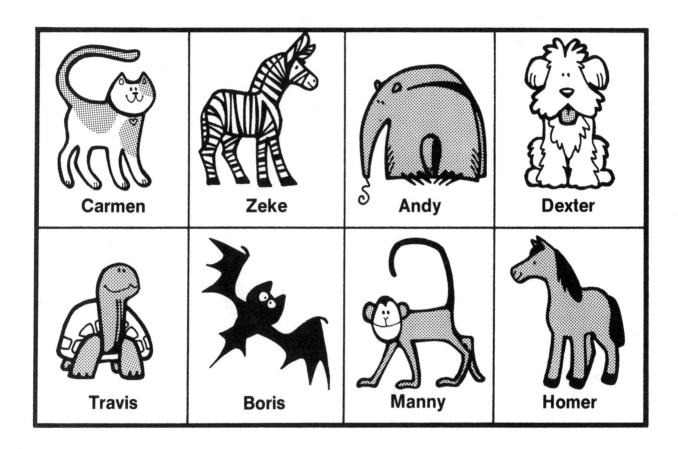

1. _____

2. _____

3. _____

4. _____

5. _____

6. _____

7. _____

8. _____

Name _____

Rhyme Time

Draw a picture of each rhyme.

a snake with a rake	**a clown upside down**	**a bat with a hat**
a pie in the sky	**a pig with a wig**	**a flower in the shower**
a hen with a pen	**a bug on my mug**	**a dog on a log**

Name _____

Hat Happenings

Choose one hat below and decide who wears it.
Draw a large picture of the hat you chose.
Under your picture, write a sentence or two about the person who wears that hat.
Add your picture and sentences to our Hat Happenings bulletin board.

Spelling Riddle

To answer this riddle, underline the correct spelling of each word.

Find the letter in front of the correct spelling, and write it on the numbered line below.

The first one has been done for you.

Where does a lamb go when it needs a haircut?

1.	r	throot	(b)	throat	g	throte
2.	e	cleen	i	klean	a	clean
3.	a	turtle	d	tirtle	e	turtel
4.	o	koast	k	coest	b	coast
5.	e	whool	a	whole	p	whule
6.	t	strenth	u	strinth	a	strength
7.	g	enuff	s	enough	k	enoff
8.	o	alreddy	b	allready	h	already
9.	a	inviet	c	invit	o	invite
10.	p	squeak	k	squeek	t	skweke

t o t h e b __ __ __ __
  1 2 3 4 5 6 7 8 9 10

Name _____

Create a Word

Make up a new word. (Check in the dictionary to be sure that your word is *not* listed.)

Write your word in large letters across the top of a piece of white paper.

Write the correct part of speech *(noun, verb, adjective,* or *adverb)* for your word.

Draw a picture of your word.

Write a definition for your word or tell what it means in one or two sentences.

Use your word in a sentence and underline your new word.

readybed
noun

a bed that is always ready for you
You don't need to wait for a <u>readybed</u> to be turned down.

SPACE RACE

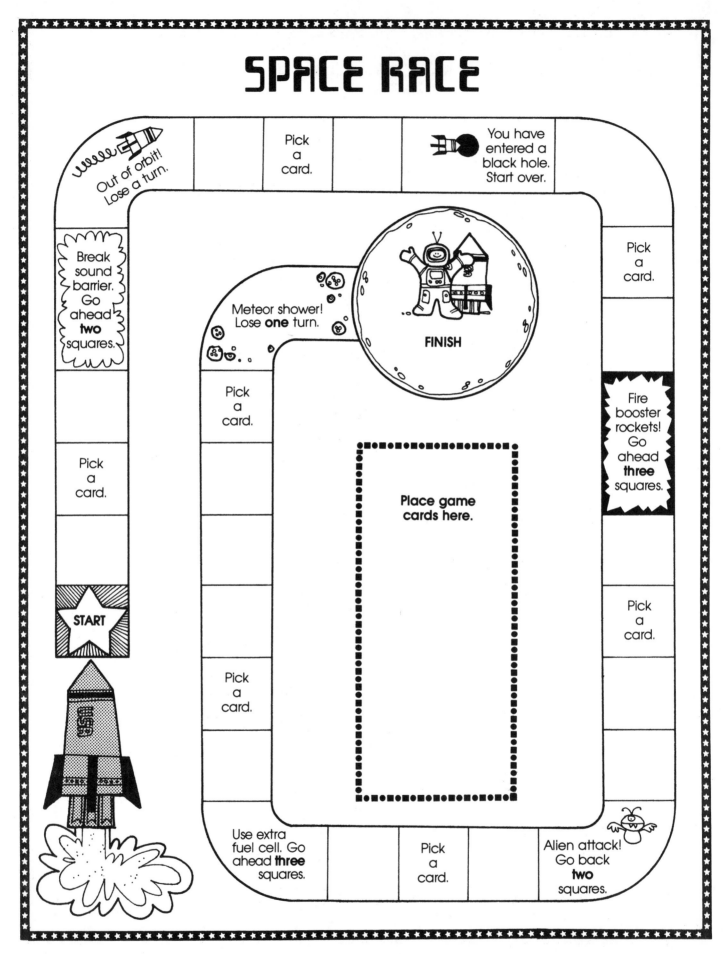

Out of orbit! Lose a turn.

Pick a card.

You have entered a black hole. Start over.

Break sound barrier. Go ahead **two** squares.

Pick a card.

Meteor shower! Lose **ONE** turn.

FINISH

Pick a card.

Fire booster rockets! Go ahead **three** squares.

Pick a card.

Place game cards here.

START

Pick a card.

Pick a card.

Use extra fuel cell. Go ahead **three** squares.

Pick a card.

Alien attack! Go back **two** squares.

The Primary Teacher's Pet
©1984 — The Learning Works, Inc.

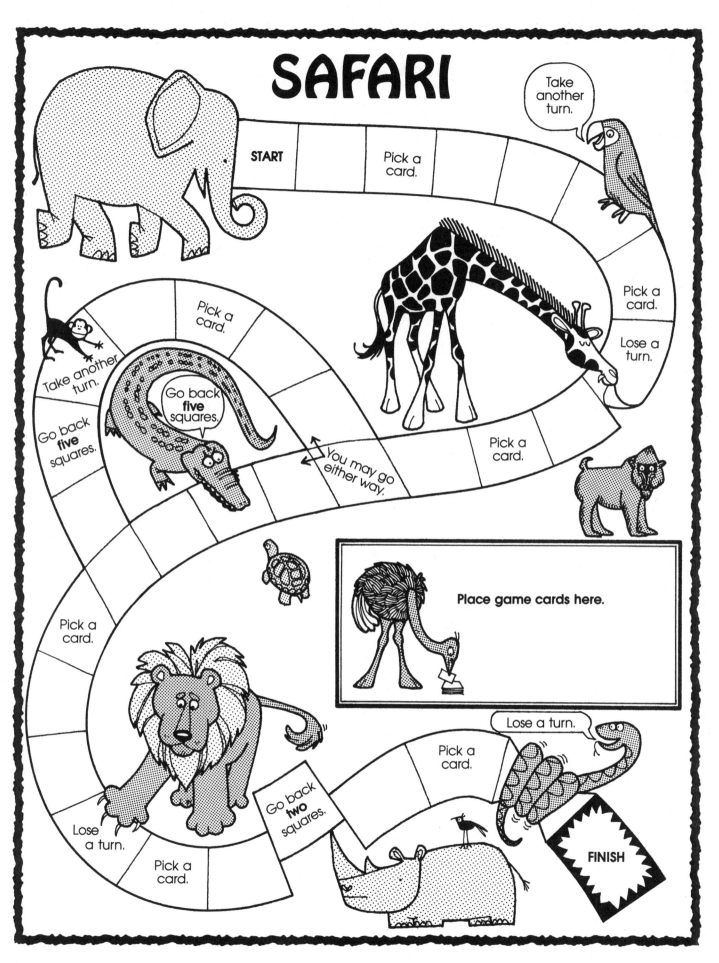

Fill-in Game Cards

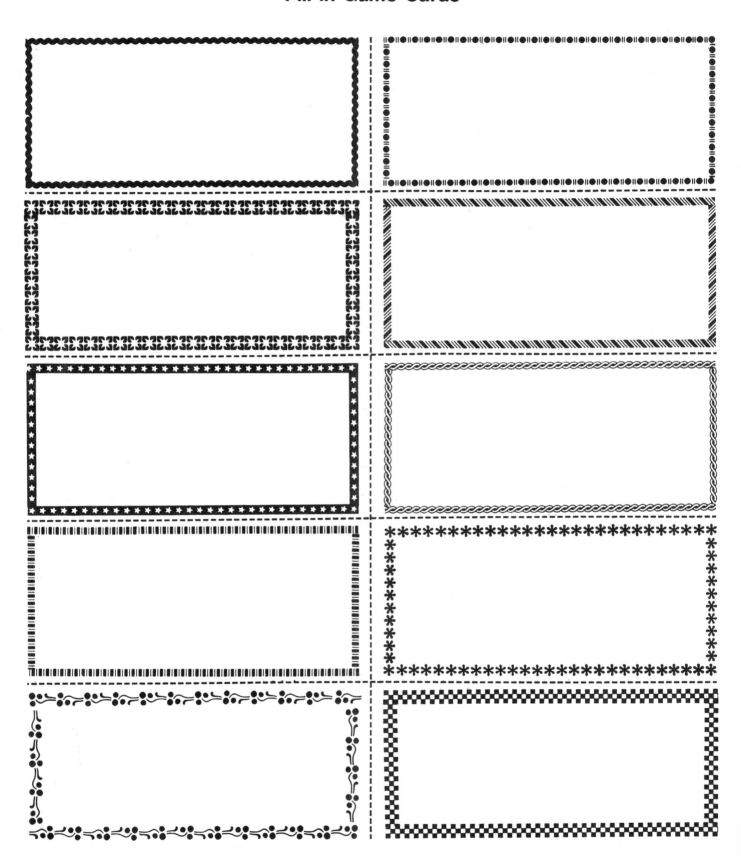

Math

Addition Table

+	0	1	2	3	4	5	6	7	8	9	10
0	0	1	2	3	4	5	6	7	8	9	10
1	1	2	3	4	5	6	7	8	9	10	11
2	2	3	4	5	6	7	8	9	10	11	12
3	3	4	5	6	7	8	9	10	11	12	13
4	4	5	6	7	8	9	10	11	12	13	14
5	5	6	7	8	9	10	11	12	13	14	15
6	6	7	8	9	10	11	12	13	14	15	16
7	7	8	9	10	11	12	13	14	15	16	17
8	8	9	10	11	12	13	14	15	16	17	18
9	9	10	11	12	13	14	15	16	17	18	19
10	10	11	12	13	14	15	16	17	18	19	20

Name _____

Blank Addition Table

+	0	1	2	3	4	5	6	7	8	9	10
0											
1											
2											
3											
4											
5											
6											
7											
8											
9											
10											

Multiplication Table

×	0	1	2	3	4	5	6	7	8	9	10
0	0	0	0	0	0	0	0	0	0	0	0
1	0	1	2	3	4	5	6	7	8	9	10
2	0	2	4	6	8	10	12	14	16	18	20
3	0	3	6	9	12	15	18	21	24	27	30
4	0	4	8	12	16	20	24	28	32	36	40
5	0	5	10	15	20	25	30	35	40	45	50
6	0	6	12	18	24	30	36	42	48	54	60
7	0	7	14	21	28	35	42	49	56	63	70
8	0	8	16	24	32	40	48	56	64	72	80
9	0	9	18	27	36	45	54	63	72	81	90
10	0	10	20	30	40	50	60	70	80	90	100

Name _____

Blank Multiplication Table

✕	0	1	2	3	4	5	6	7	8	9	10
0											
1											
2											
3											
4											
5											
6											
7											
8											
9											
10											

Time Chart

1 minute	=	60 seconds
1 hour	=	60 minutes
1 day	=	24 hours
1 week	=	7 days
1 month	=	28, 29, 30, or 31 days
1 year	=	365 or 366 days
1 year	=	52 weeks
1 year	=	12 months
1 decade	=	10 years
1 century	=	100 years

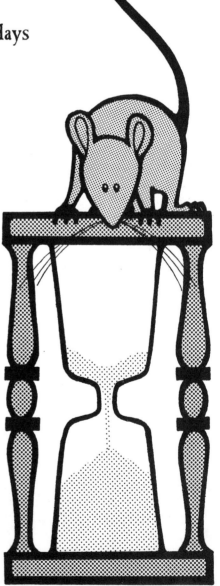

The Primary Teacher's Pet
©1984 — The Learning Works, Inc.

Name _____

It's About Time

_____ _____ _____

_____ _____ _____

_____ _____ _____ _____

Tables of Weights and Measures

English Units

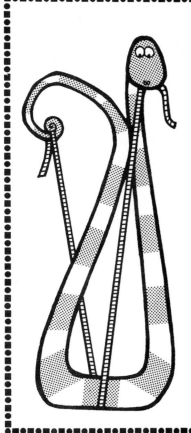

Length

1 foot (ft.) = 12 inches (in.)
1 yard (yd.) = 3 feet
1 mile (mi.) = 5,280 feet
1 mile (mi.) = 1,760 yards

Weight

1 pound (lb.) = 16 ounces (oz.)
1 ton (tn.) = 2,000 pounds

Liquid Volume

1 pint (pt.) = 2 cups
1 quart (qt.) = 2 pints
1 gallon (gal.) = 4 quarts

Metric Units

Length

1 meter (m) = 100 centimeters (cm)
1 kilometer (km) = 1,000 meters

Weight

1 kilogram (kg) = 1,000 grams (g)

Liquid Volume

1 liter (l) = 1,000 milliliters (ml)
1 kiloliter (kl) = 1,000 liters

The Primary Teacher's Pet
©1984 — The Learning Works, Inc.

Money

Auntie Anteater's Addition

Help Auntie Anteater find the sums.

1. 3 + 2	**2.** 7 + 4	**3.** 6 + 6	**4.** 8 + 7
5. 5 + 4	**6.** 2 + 9	**7.** 7 + 5	**8.** 6 + 8
9. 11 + 4	**10.** 13 + 6	**11.** 15 + 2	**12.** 14 + 3
13. 23 + 8	**14.** 14 + 8	**15.** 26 + 6	**16.** 45 + 9

Name _____

Super Snake Subtraction

Find the differences.
Then color your answers on the snake.

1. 14 − 9	**2.** 10 − 6	**3.** 12 − 5
4. 15 − 7	**5.** 14 − 8	**6.** 13 − 3
7. 20 − 6	**8.** 22 − 4	**9.** 18 − 7
10. 31 − 16	**11.** 52 − 28	**12.** 40 − 32

Name _____

Monster Math

Work the problems, and write your answers on the lines.

1. Boris went to the dentist to have his fangs filled. The dentist filled two cavities and charged Boris $42 each. How much did Boris pay the dentist? _____

2. Mighty Monster eats mushy marshmallows. There were fifty marshmallows in the giant economy size bag. The monster ate thirteen of them. How many marshmallows were left? _____

3. The monsters meet monthly on Monday. If six monsters come from Maple Lane, eight come from Main Street, and seven come from Myrtle Road, how many monsters come in all? _____

4. One morning fifteen gorbles were sitting on a fence. After Boris left, there were only six. How many gorbles did Boris eat for breakfast? _____

5. Hessie is a monster covered with scales. She likes to paint them bright pink. If she paints twelve scales on Monday, two on Tuesday, six on Wednesday, five on Thursday, and seven on Friday, how many scales does she paint in all? _____

Social Studies

Map of the United States

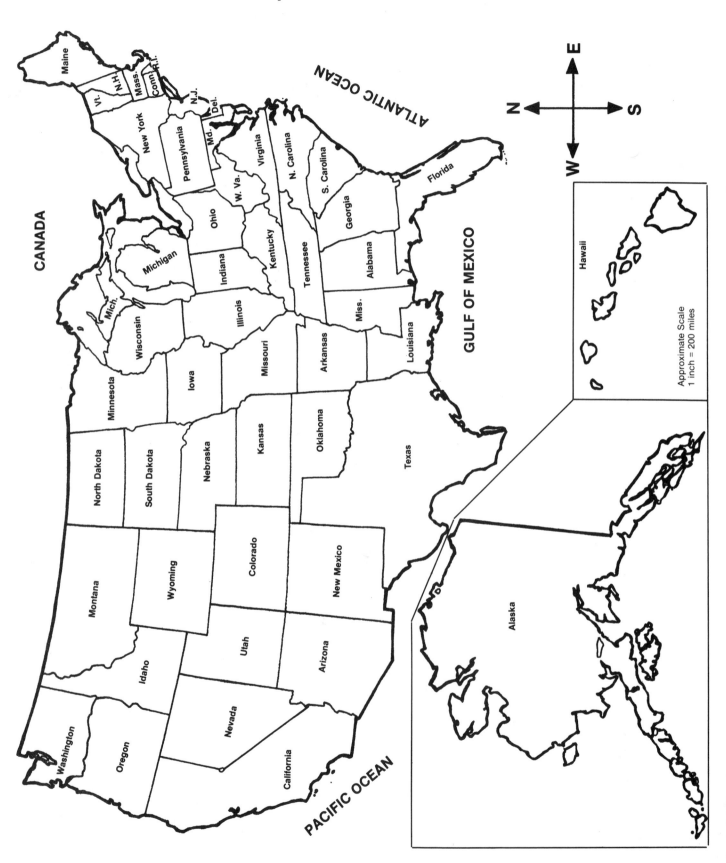

Name _____

Map Quiz

Look at the map of the United States on page 110.
Use it to answer these questions.

1. Which is the largest state? _____

2. What state is south of Georgia? _____

3. What state is north of Oregon? _____

4. Which state is made up of many islands? _____

5. Which state is directly west of North Carolina? _____

6. How many states border Idaho? _____

7. Which state is farther north, Colorado or Louisiana? _____

8. Which state is farther east, Missouri or Kentucky? _____

9. Which state is directly east of Arizona? _____

10. Which state is directly south of South Dakota? _____

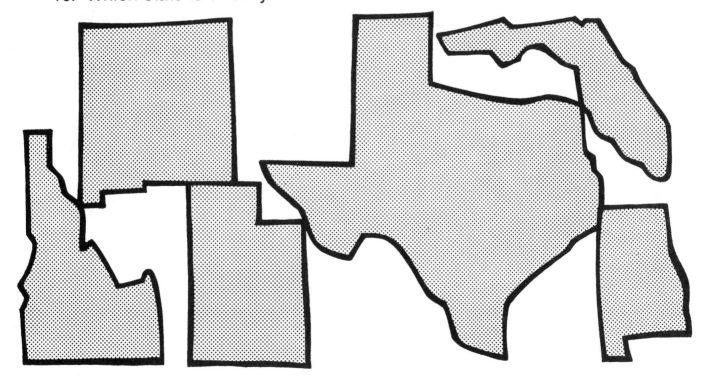

Name _____

Make a Map

Symbols are simple shapes or pictures that stand for other things. Symbols are used on maps to mark special places and to stand for special buildings. Here are some symbols that you may find on a map.

airport	✈	hospital	⌂	railroad	┼┼┼┼
bridge	⌒	island	⟨⌃⌃⟩	river	〜〜
church	⌂	lake	▱	school	⌐
city	●	library	⌂	street	—
hills	⌢⌢	mountains	∧∧	tunnel	⌐⌐⌐

Create your own town by adding six or more of these symbols to the map outline below.

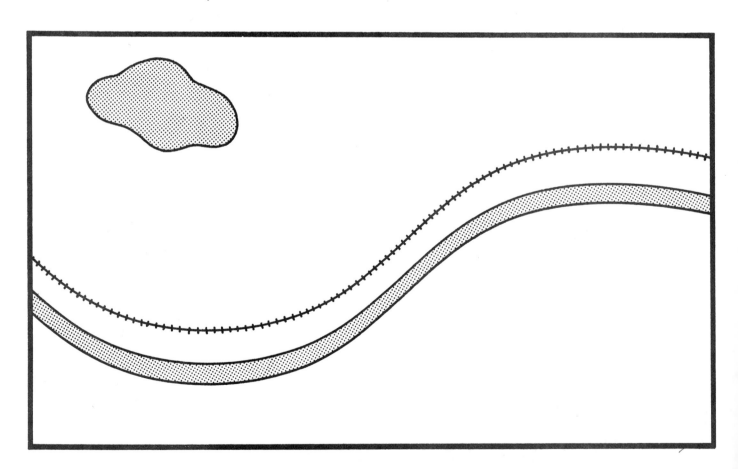

What is the name of your town? _____

Name _____

North, South, East, or West?

Some maps have a **compass rose** on them to show you which way is north, which way is south, which way is east, and which way is west. These directions are marked by letters on the compass rose. **N** stands for **north**, **S** stands for **south**, **E** stands for **east**, and **W** stands for **west**.

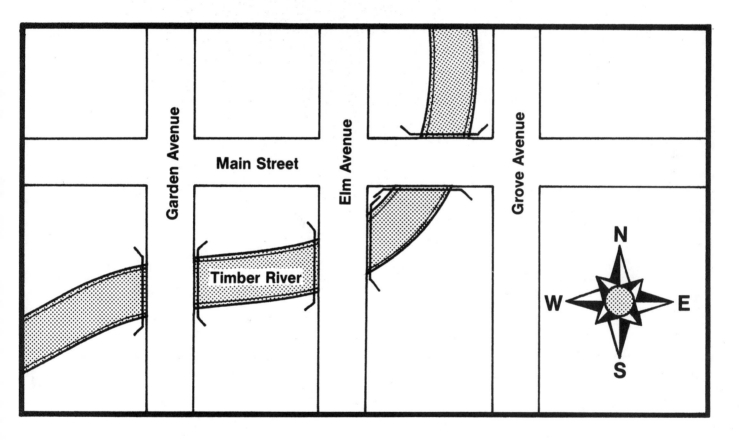

Use the compass rose on this map to tell you the direction words you need to complete the statements.

1. Grove Avenue is _____ of Elm Avenue.

2. Garden Avenue is _____ of Elm Avenue.

3. Main Street runs _____ and _____ .

4. Elm Avenue runs _____ and _____ .

5. The Timber River is _____ of Grove Avenue.

The Primary Teacher's Pet
©1984 — The Learning Works, Inc.

Name _____

My Family Tree

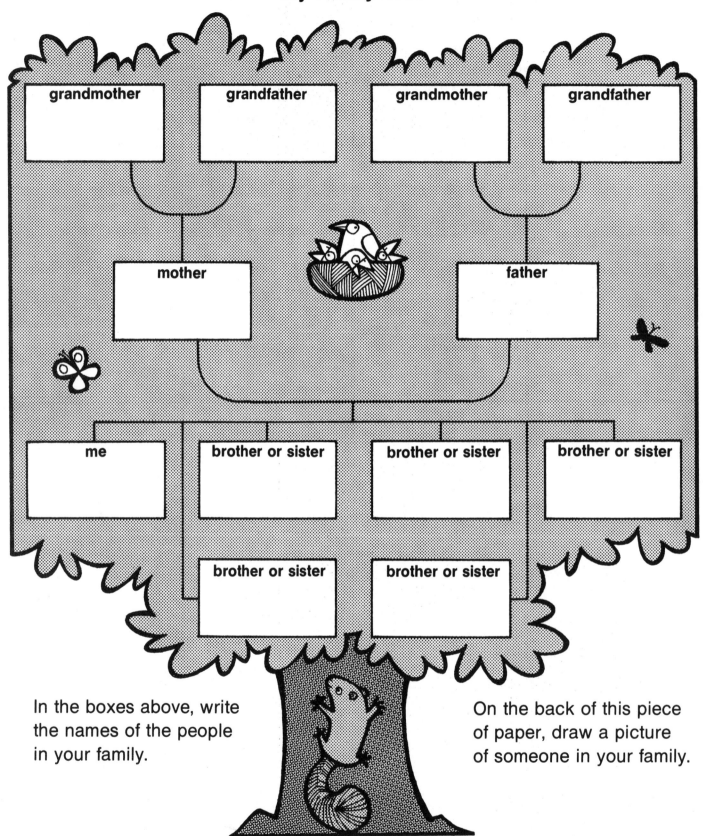

grandmother

grandfather

grandmother

grandfather

mother

father

me

brother or sister

brother or sister

brother or sister

brother or sister

brother or sister

In the boxes above, write the names of the people in your family.

On the back of this piece of paper, draw a picture of someone in your family.

Name _____

Who's in the Zoo?

Use this grid to answer the questions on page 116.

Who's in the Zoo?
(continued)

Sometimes people use a **letter-number grid** to tell where a place is or to find something on a map. First, a mapmaker draws a grid over the map. Next, he letters the squares across the top and numbers the squares down the side. Then, each square has a letter-number address. People who read the map can use this address to tell someone where a place is or to find something they want.

Use the grid on page 115 to answer these questions. The first one has been done for you.

1. In what square is the entrance to this zoo? _____ **A5** _____

2. Where would you find the monkey cage? _____

3. In what two squares are the tigers? _____ and _____

4. Where are the seals? _____

5. Where is the lunch stand? _____

6. In what square are the bears? _____

7. Where are the birds? _____

8. In what square is the popcorn stand? _____

9. Where is the lion cage? _____

10. In what two squares are the elephants? _____ and _____

Community Helpers

teacher

waitress

crossing guard

farm worker

Community Helpers
(continued)

architect

cook

mechanic

librarian

Check out books here.

Social Studies
©1984 — The Learning Works, Inc.

Community Helpers
(continued)

plumber

veterinarian

gardener

barber

Community Helpers
(continued)

mail carrier

janitor

construction worker

doctor

Community Helpers
(continued)

electrician

computer programmer

police officer

artist

Community Helpers
(continued)

house painter

fire fighter

carpenter

sales clerk

1295

SALE

Transportation Time

Communication Collection

Science

Your Eyes

Your eyes send picture messages to your brain. When your eyes are open, rays of light come through the small black hole in the center of each eye called the **pupil**. These light rays pass through a **lens**, which focuses them. They make a picture of what you see on the back of your eyeball, which is called the **retina**. This picture is carried by a special **nerve** to your brain. Your brain decides what the picture is, what it means, and what you should do about it.

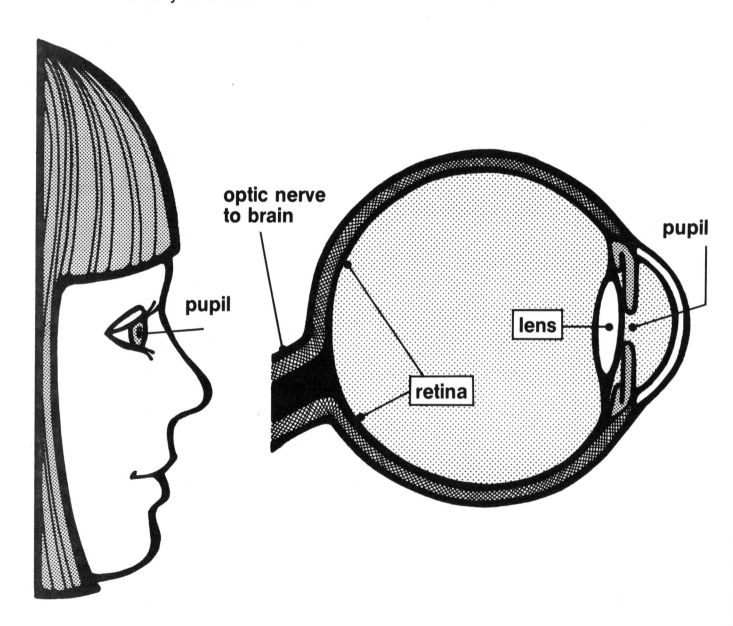

optic nerve
to brain

pupil

pupil

lens

retina

The Primary Teacher's Pet
©1984 — The Learning Works, Inc.

Your Ears

Your ears send sound messages to your brain. Sounds make the air ripple, or **vibrate** in waves. Though you cannot see these waves, they spread out in circles from the sound that makes them like the waves in a pond when you drop a rock into it.

The outer part of your ear, called the **pinna**, gathers sound waves that are in the air. They go inside your ear. They bump against your **eardrum** and make it wiggle, or vibrate.

When the eardrum vibrates, it makes three tiny bones inside your ear vibrate also. In turn, these bones make a **liquid** in your ear vibrate. Hairlike **nerve ends** in this liquid feel these vibrations and carry them to your brain. Your brain decides what sound you heard and whether it was noise or music.

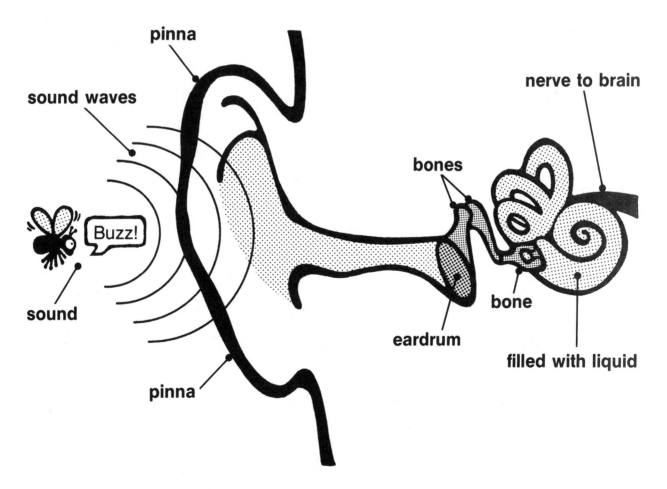

Your Bones

Your bones are the framework for your body. They hold it up, give it shape, and protect the softer parts inside.

Your body has 206 bones. The smallest one is in your ear. It is not much larger than the nail on your little finger. The largest one is your **thigh**, the part of your leg between your **knee** and your **hip**. This bone may be as much as twelve inches long—or even longer if you are very tall.

The bones in your body have special names. For example, the large bone in your thigh is a **femur** (FEE-mur). Your kneecap is called a **patella** (pa-TELL-a). And that tiny bone in your ear is called a **stirrup**, or **stapes** (STAY-peez).

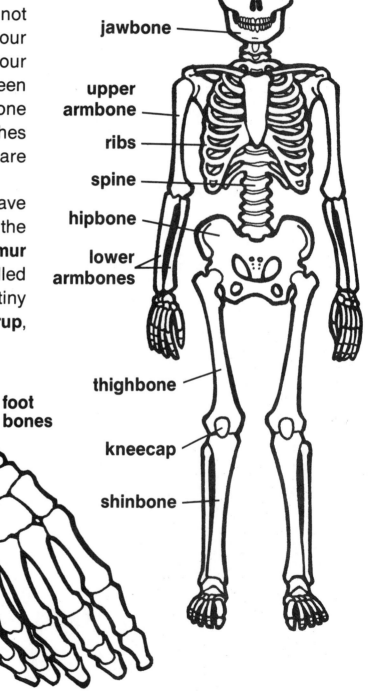

skull

jawbone

upper armbone

ribs

spine

hipbone

lower armbones

thighbone

kneecap

shinbone

hand bones

foot bones

Inside Your Body

Inside your body are many soft parts that work hard to keep you healthy and strong. These parts work even when you play. They help you get oxygen from the air you breathe. They help you get energy from the food you eat. They help you get rid of the air and food your body has used and doesn't need anymore.

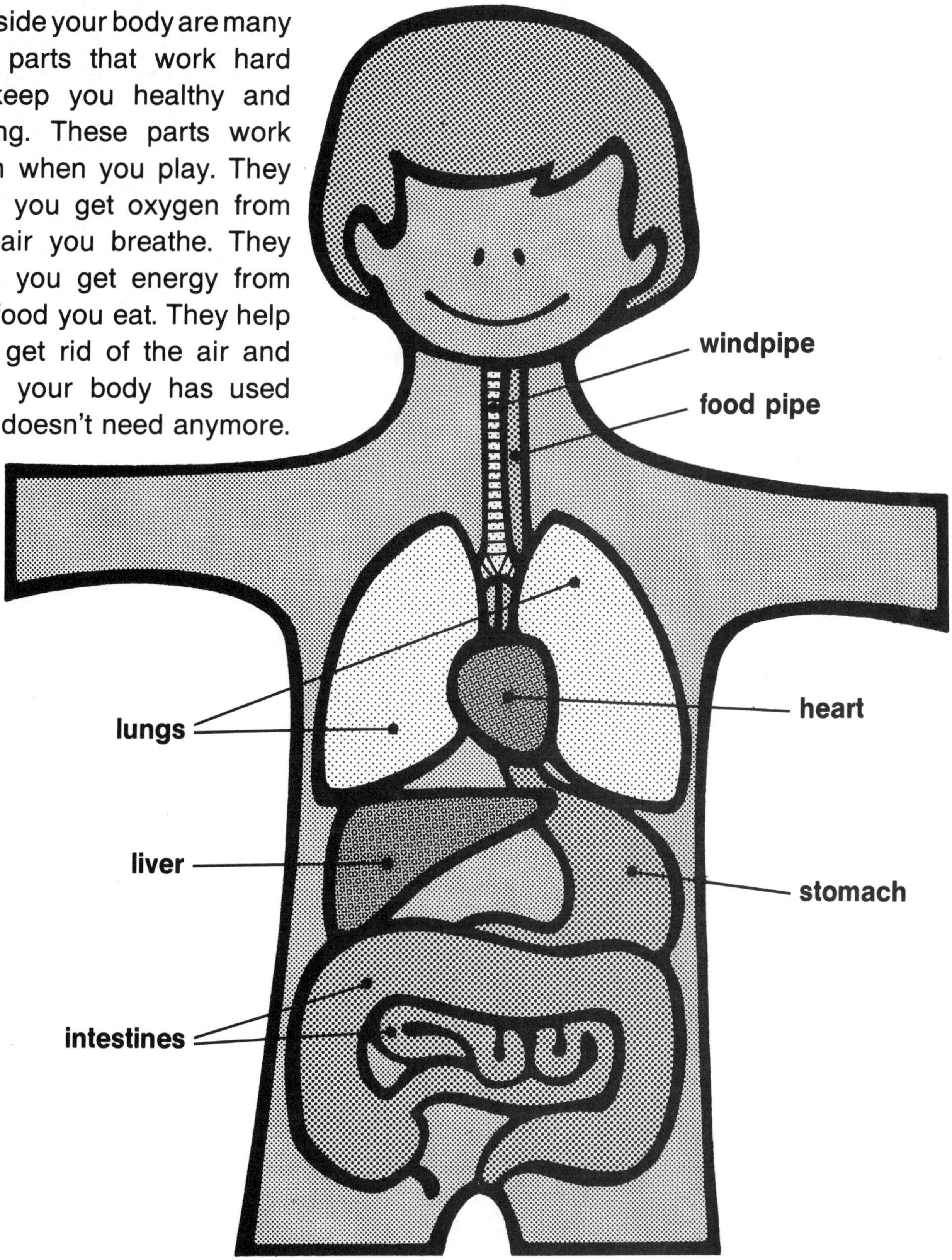

windpipe

food pipe

heart

lungs

liver

stomach

intestines

Your Teeth

Your teeth are very important. They bite, chew, and grind the food you eat. Without teeth, you could not eat apples, carrots, or nuts.

Because teeth are so important, they are built to last a long time—if you take good care of them. They are covered by **enamel** (ee-NAM-ul), a hard coating that protects them and makes them look shiny and white. Under the enamel is a layer of **dentin** (DEN-tin), which is harder than bone! Inside the dentin layer is some spongy stuff called **pulp**.

Your teeth look like they are just sitting on top of your **gums**. Really, they have **roots** that go down into your gums. These roots are held in place by **bone**. Inside each root is a **nerve**. Sometimes when you drink something very cold, these nerves make your teeth hurt. If you feel pain in a tooth at any other time, you should have it checked by your dentist.

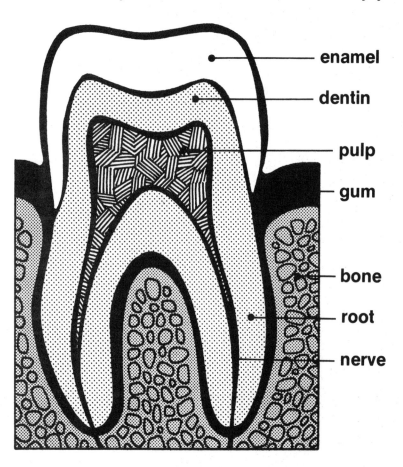

- enamel
- dentin
- pulp
- gum
- bone
- root
- nerve

The Four Food Groups

milk group

COTTAGE CHEESE

YOGURT

meat group

TUNA

SLICED BEEF

PEANUT BUTTER

bread and cereal group

fruit and vegetable group

Name _____

Marvelous Menus

A **menu** is a list of the foods served at a meal. Write menus for these three meals. Remember to choose foods from the four food groups pictured on page 131.

Breakfast

_____
_____
_____
_____
_____

Lunch

_____
_____
_____
_____

Dinner

_____
_____
_____
_____

Parts of a Plant

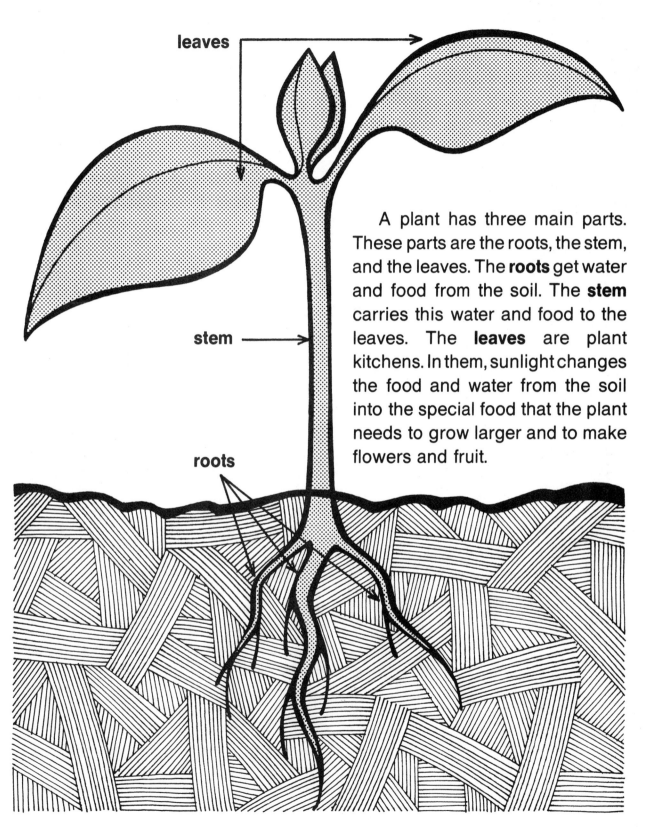

A plant has three main parts. These parts are the roots, the stem, and the leaves. The **roots** get water and food from the soil. The **stem** carries this water and food to the leaves. The **leaves** are plant kitchens. In them, sunlight changes the food and water from the soil into the special food that the plant needs to grow larger and to make flowers and fruit.

Flower Power

apple blossom	hibiscus
aster	iris
begonia	lilac
bluebell	lily
buttercup	marigold
camellia	orchid
carnation	pansy
daffodil	petunia
daisy	poppy
dandelion	rose
dogwood	snapdragon
gardenia	sunflower
geranium	sweet pea
goldenrod	tulip
heather	violet

The Primary Teacher's Pet
©1984 — The Learning Works, Inc.

Treasury of Trees

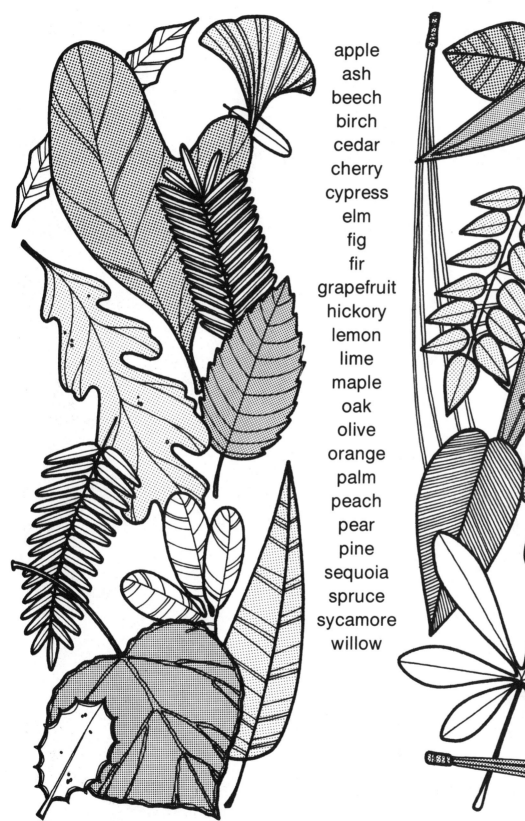
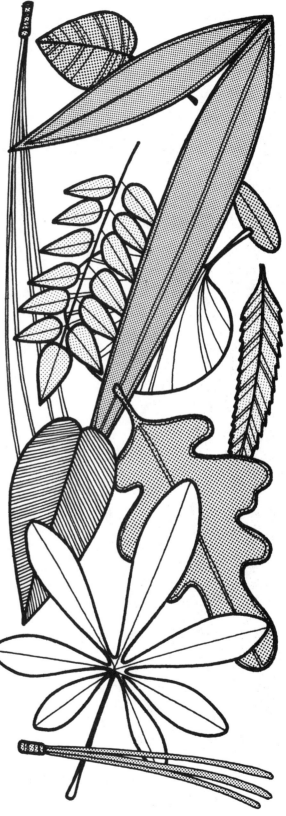

apple
ash
beech
birch
cedar
cherry
cypress
elm
fig
fir
grapefruit
hickory
lemon
lime
maple
oak
olive
orange
palm
peach
pear
pine
sequoia
spruce
sycamore
willow

Dinosaurs

iguanodon
(i-GWAN-a-don)

trachodon
(TRAK-a-don)

Dinosaurs
(continued)

stegosaurus
(steg-a-SAWR-us)

triceratops
(try-SER-a-tops)

Dinosaurs
(continued)

diplodocus
(di-PLOD-a-kus)

brachiosaurus
(brak-ee-o-SAWR-us)

Dinosaurs
(continued)

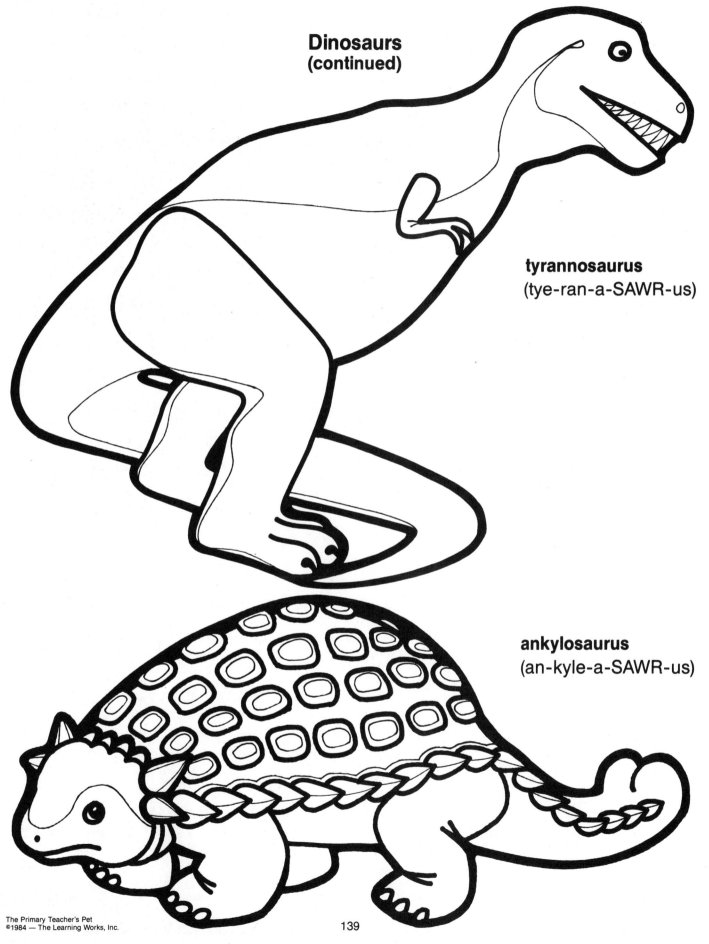

tyrannosaurus
(tye-ran-a-SAWR-us)

ankylosaurus
(an-kyle-a-SAWR-us)

Name _____

Vote for Your Favorite Dinosaur

I am **Tyrannosaurus**, the fiercest of all!
I weigh eight tons, and I'm two stories tall.
My long, strong tail can knock down a tree.
Don't you think you should vote for me?

I am **Brachiosaurus**! Vote for me, instead.
My eyes and nose are on top of my head.
The rest of me hides in the deep green sea.
When an enemy comes, he can't see me.

I am **Triceratops**, the best of all.
My skull is longer than you are tall.
I can't move fast, but I'm very strong;
And my horns are almost three feet long!

I am **Iguanodon**. Here's what I can do:
I can walk on four legs, or walk on two.
In a squishy swamp, four are best, I've found;
But I walk on two when I'm on dry ground.

I am **Diplodocus**, the longest dinosaur.
I look like Brachiosaurus, but he weighs more.
My mouth is tiny, and my teeth are too.
I eat only plants. I'd never eat you!

I am a super **Stegosaurus** with spikes on my tail.
They're two feet long and sharp as a nail.
These plates keep my enemies off my back
While I'm eating some swamp plants for a snack.

I am **Trachodon**, a duck-billed beast;
And prehistoric plants are my favorite feast.
My mouth has many, many teeth, you know —
A thousand above and a thousand below!

I look like a tank. I'm an **Ankylosaurus.**
We aren't very big, but the others ignore us.
We have so many plates that there's no place to bite,
And this tail is a dangerous weapon to fight.

This page has been adapted from *Pint-Size Puppet Projects,* written and illustrated by Beverly Armstrong (Santa Barbara, Calif.: The Learning Works, 1978).

Name _____

What Does a Computer Look Like?

A computer looks like a televison set and a typewriter put together. But that's only two parts of the computer. Most computers have five parts. These parts are the

1. **video screen**, which looks like a television set
2. **central processing unit**, which is inside the television set
3. **keyboard**, which looks like a typewriter
4. **disk drive**
5. **printer**

Together, they are called the **hardware**.

Color this picture
of computer hardware.

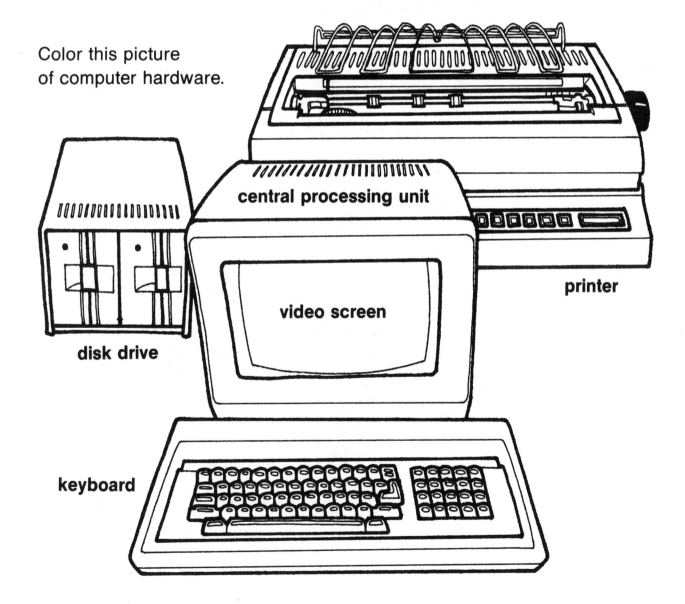

What Is Computer Software?

Computer software is any program used on a computer. Software tells the computer what to do. Software may be stored on

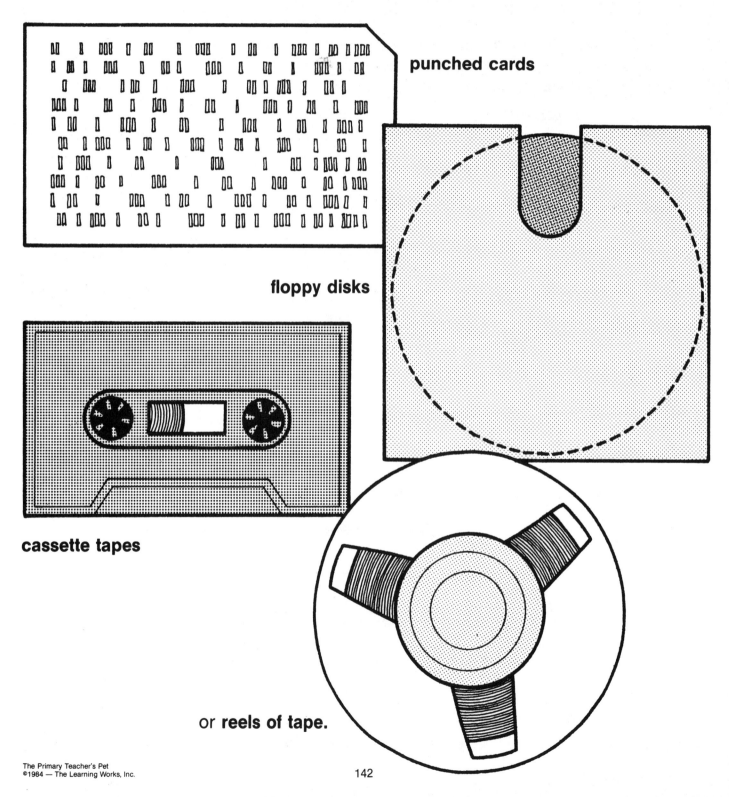

punched cards

floppy disks

cassette tapes

or **reels of tape.**

Computer Talk

BASIC	Beginner's All-purpose Symbolic Instruction Code, a computer language
bit	a storage cell in a computer's memory
byte	a group of bits
cartridge	box or case that contains a cassette tape
central processing unit (CPU)	the part of a computer that works with and stores data
chip	thumbnail-sized integrated electrical circuit used to build the processing and memory units of today's computers
code	a group of lines, letters, or symbols that can be read and understood by a computer
computer	a programmable electronic machine that works with data
cursor	a lighted or blinking shape on the video screen which marks the spot where a message will be printed or a symbol or color will appear if a key on the keyboard is pressed
data	numbers and information that are given to a computer
erase	to rub out, get rid of, or do away with
floppy disk	a disk that looks like a 45-rpm record on which programs can be stored

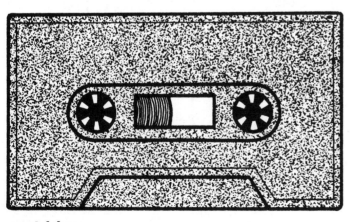

cartridge

chip

code 7540 49076

More Computer Talk

flow chart	a graphic outline of the steps that are necessary to do a job or to solve a problem
input	the information that is put into a computer
keyboard	the piece of computer hardware that looks like a typewriter and is used to give information to the computer
memory	the capacity of a computer to store data
output	the answer, response, or results presented by a computer
printer	the piece of computer hardware that types printed output, or printout
printout	computer output that is typed, or printed out, on paper
program	a series or set of instructions given to a computer in a language that it can understand
programmer	a person who gives instructions to a computer
video screen	the piece of computer hardware that looks like a television set and displays symbols, words, numbers, or colors

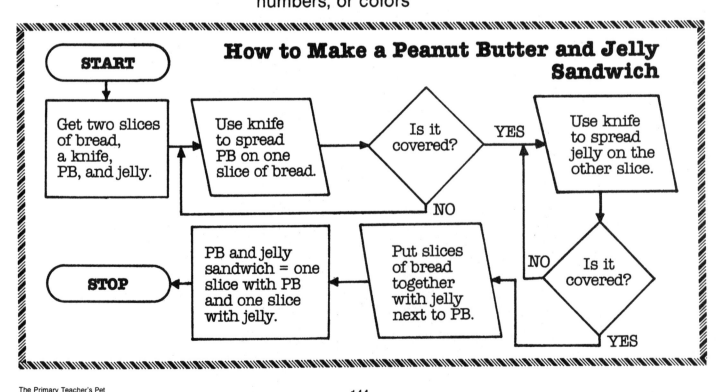

How to Make a Peanut Butter and Jelly Sandwich

Awards

SUPER STUDENT

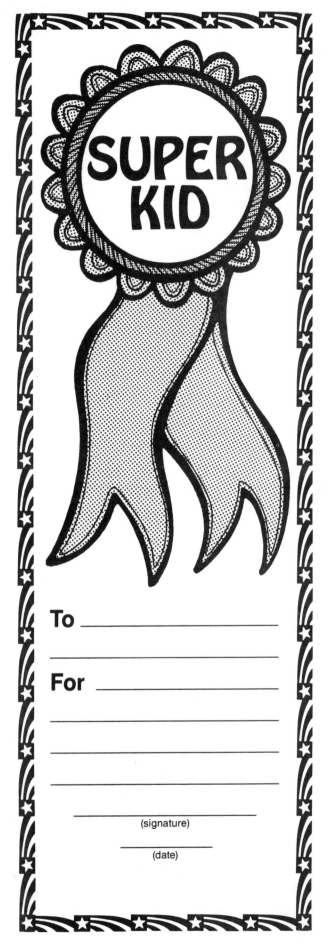

To _____

_____

For _____

_____

_____

_____

_____
(signature)

_____
(date)

To _____

_____

For _____

_____
(signature)

_____
(date)

The Primary Teacher's Pet
©1984 — The Learning Works, Inc.

The Primary Teacher's Pet
©1984 — The Learning Works, Inc.

ENORMOUS EFFORT AWARD

To _____

For _____ Date _____

The Primary Teacher's Pet
©1984 — The Learning Works, Inc.

YOU'RE SHOWING
BIG
IMPROVEMENT!

To _____

For _____

_____
(signature)

_____
(date)

The Primary Teacher's Pet
©1984 — The Learning Works, Inc.

CLEAN DESK AWARD

To _____

_____

For _____

_____

_____   _____
(signature)   (date)

The Primary Teacher's Pet
©1984 — The Learning Works, Inc.

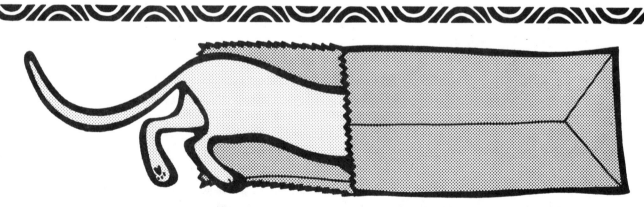

CERTIFICATE OF CURIOSITY

To _____

For _____

Signature _____

Date _____

The Primary Teacher's Pet
©1984 — The Learning Works, Inc.

(name)

CAN FOLLOW DIRECTIONS, AND I'M GLAD!

(signature)

(date)

SUPER LISTENER

To

From

Date

GREAT BEHAVIOR AWARD

To _____

For _____

From _____

Date _____

The Primary Teacher's Pet
©1984 — The Learning Works, Inc.

GOOD SPORT CERTIFICATE

To _____

For _____

From _____ Date _____

The Primary Teacher's Pet
©1984 — The Learning Works, Inc.

GRRREAT READING!

To _____

For _____

_____

From _____

_____

Date _____

BOOK REPORT BALLOON-O-GRAM

To _____

For _____

_____

_____

From _____

Date _____

WISE SPELLER AWARD

To _____

_____

For _____

_____

_____

From _____

Date _____

PERFECT PRINTER AWARD

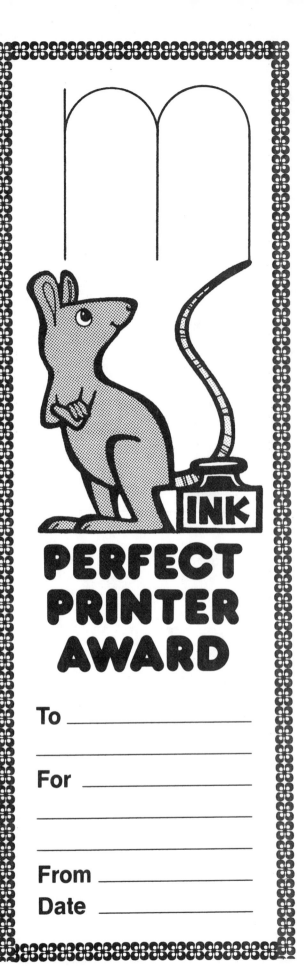

To _____

_____

For _____

_____

_____

From _____

Date _____

1 2 3 4 5 6 7 8 9
10 11 12 13 14 15 16 17 18
19 20 21 22 23 24 25 26 27
28 29 30 31 32 33 34 35 36
37 38 39
40

INCREDIBLE COUNTER AWARD

To _____

_____

For _____

_____

From _____

_____

Date _____

MATH MAGICIAN AWARD

To _____

_____

For _____

_____

From _____

_____

Date _____

MAD ADDER AWARD

To _____

_____

For _____

From _____

Date _____

The Primary Teacher's Pet
©1984 — The Learning Works, Inc.

SUBTRACTION SUPERSTAR ★

To _____

_____

For _____

_____

From _____

Date _____

The Primary Teacher's Pet
©1984 — The Learning Works, Inc.

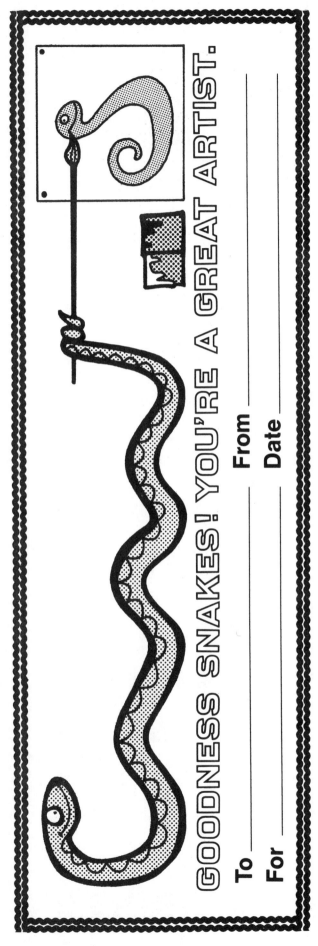

GOODNESS SNAKES! YOU'RE A GREAT ARTIST.

To _____

For _____

From _____

Date _____

CREATIVE KID CERTIFICATE

Given to _____

For _____

By _____

On _____
                    (signature)   (date)

COMMUNITY HELPER EXPERT

To _____

For _____

_____

From _____

Date _____

SUPER SCIENTIST

To _____

For _____

_____

From _____

Date _____

The Primary Teacher's Pet
©1984 — The Learning Works, Inc.

The Primary Teacher's Pet
©1984 — The Learning Works, Inc.

Art and Holiday Happenings

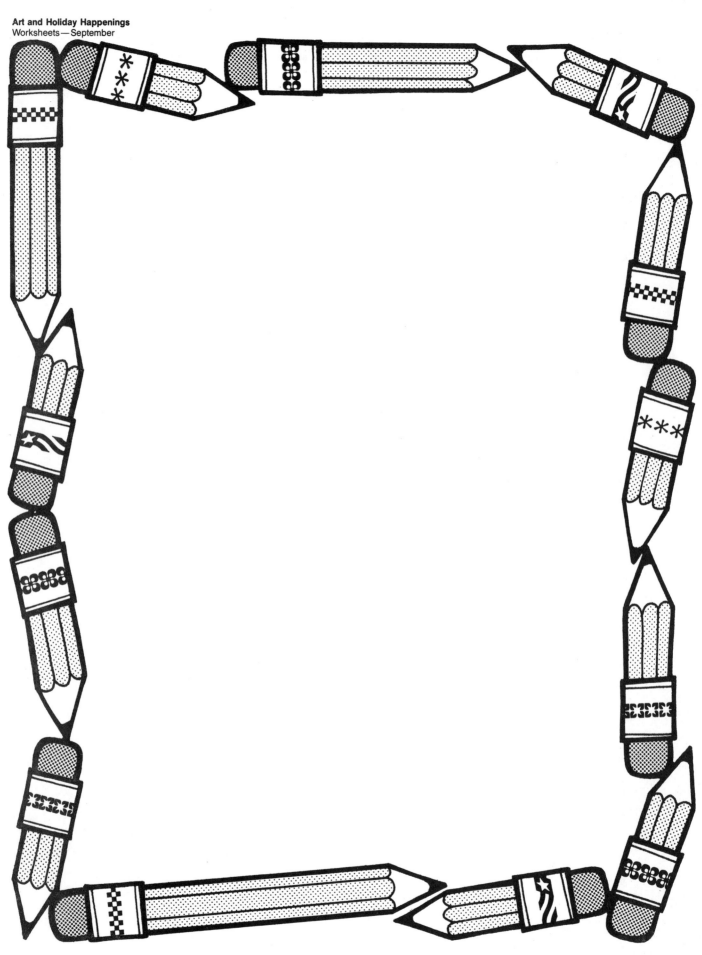

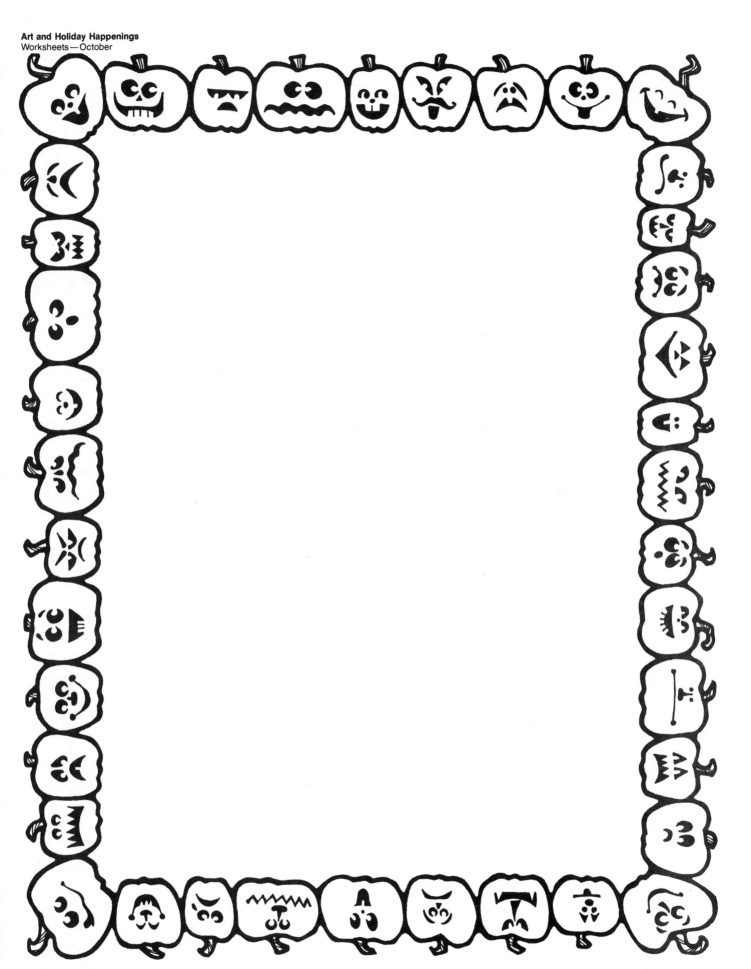

The Primary Teacher's Pet
©1984 — The Learning Works, Inc.

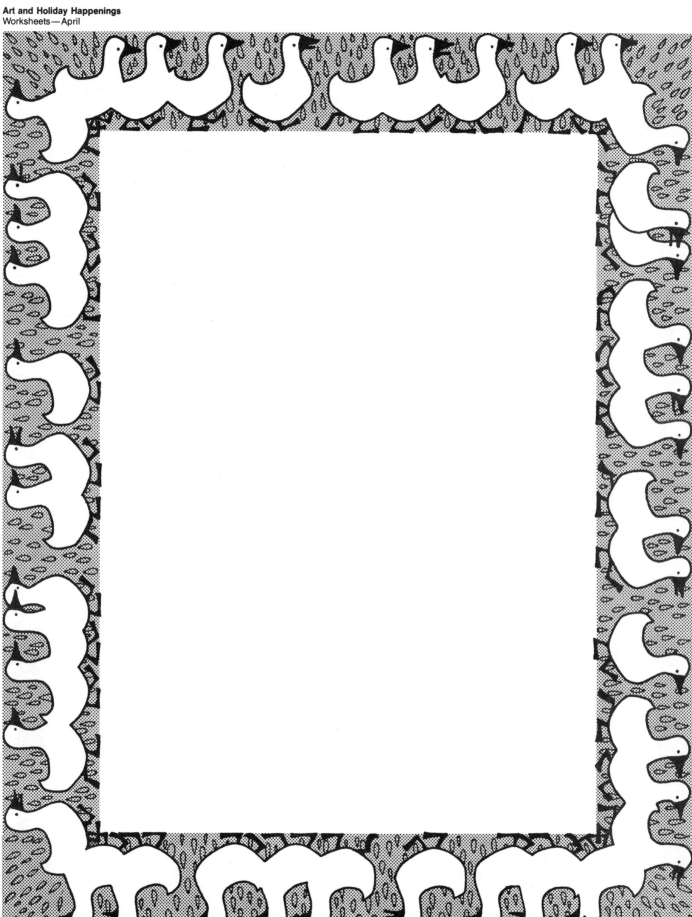

The Primary Teacher's Pet
©1984 — The Learning Works, Inc.

Clip Art

On pages 169-181 are theme-related drawings that you can use to create your own activity cards, announcements, awards, contracts, flyers, game boards, invitations, name tags, and programs, and to add a touch of whimsy to worksheets and tests. These drawings are grouped by subject or theme.

Although this art is theme-related, it is readily adaptable to any classroom occasion or school year event. All you need to do is duplicate the page (so you can use the clip art on the other side later), cut out the drawing you wish to use, attach it to the sheet you intend to decorate, and reproduce the sheet with art in place.

With the help of an opaque projector or squared paper, you can enlarge clip art drawings for other applications. For example, you can make them large enough for effective use on bulletin boards, posters, and signs. You can also use them as patterns for book covers, borders, greeting cards, and other student- or teacher-made art.

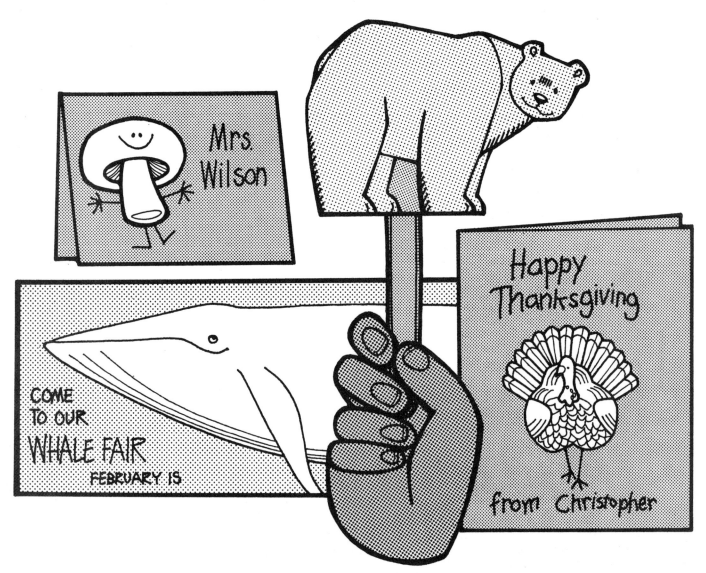

Farm Animals

Zoo Animals

Water Animals

Amphibians and Reptiles

Garden Creatures

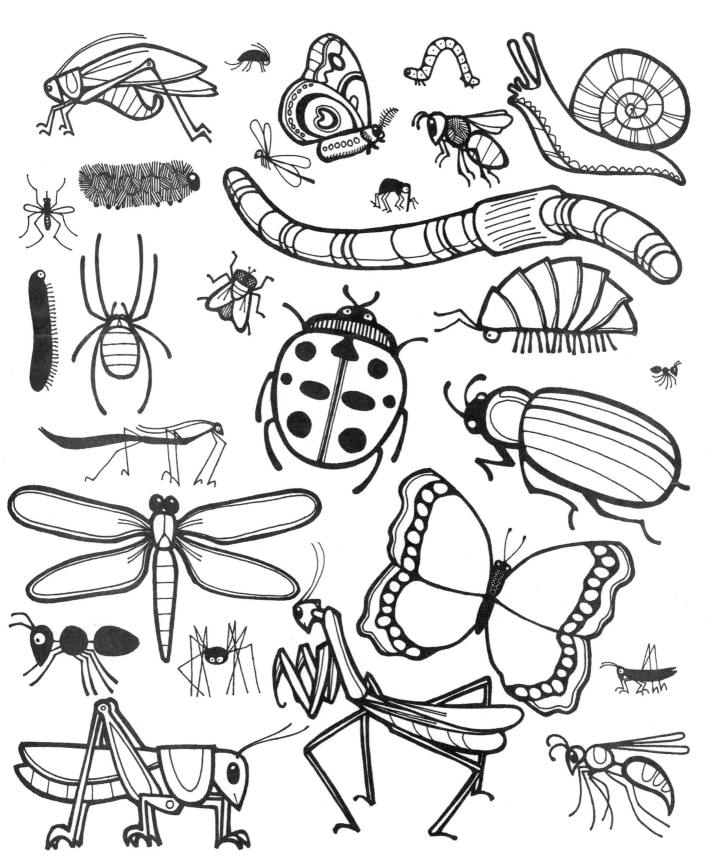

Fruits

Vegetables

Sports Shorts

On Stage

Happy Holidays

Happy Holidays
(continued)

Happy Holidays
(continued)

The Primary Teacher's Pet
©1984 — The Learning Works, Inc.

Space Race

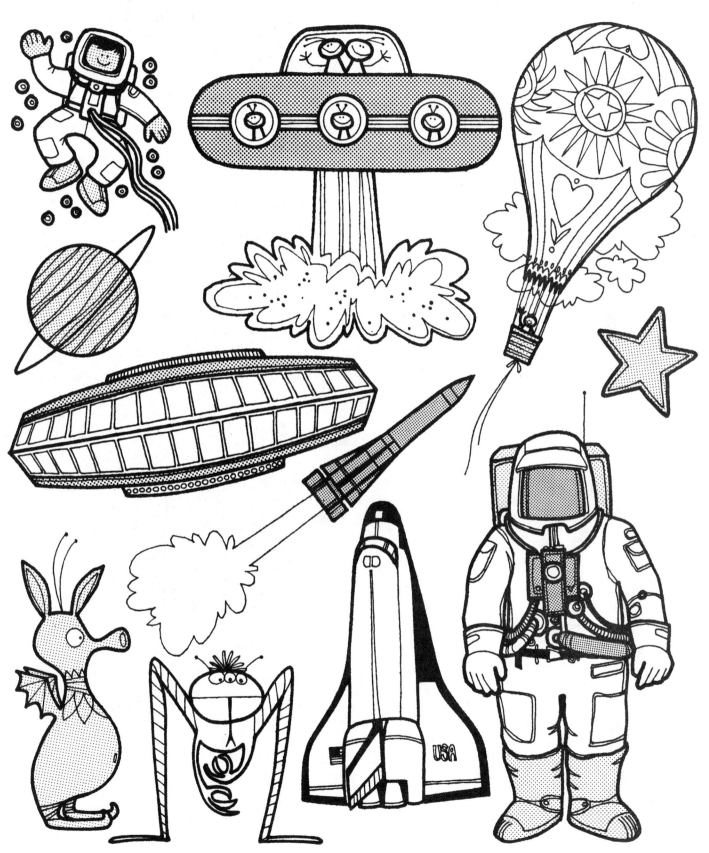

Borders

Borders cover rough edges, make any display look more finished, and add a seasonal or holiday touch to subject matter bulletin boards. They can easily be cut paper-doll style from folded lengths of paper or fabric.

Colored construction paper is probably the most widely used border material; however, for interesting effects, try felt, foil, gift wrap, newspaper, patterned shelf paper, plaid or print fabric, or wallpaper. For variety, combine and overlap borders of different but compatible shapes or borders of the same shape cut from paper or fabric of different shades or colors.

To create a border, first decide whether you intend to run bands across the top and bottom, down the sides, or entirely around your board. Measure this distance in inches. Divide the total distance in inches by the length of a single strip of paper or fabric, also in inches, to determine how many strips you need. Cut that number of strips.

Fold each strip in half and then in half again. Photocopy or trace any of the patterns on pages 183-191. Position the pattern on your folded paper or fabric as shown, draw around it with a pencil or chalk, and cut out the resulting shape. Carefully unfold the strip.

The borders on the following pages have been designed to make efficient use of a 12-inch-by-18-inch piece of construction paper. Most of them can be cut from either a folded 12-inch strip or a folded 18-inch strip. Note the dimensions given beside each pattern.

Acorns and Leaves

Acorns

Cut from 3-inch-by-18-inch strips folded to be 3-inch-by-4½-inch rectangles. For best results, place the stem edge on the thick fold. Vary by using a felt-tipped pen to darken the caps and stems or by cutting them from paper of a darker shade and gluing or stapling them to the border.

thick fold

Grape Leaves

Cut from 4-inch-by-18-inch strips folded to be 4-inch-by-4½-inch rectangles. For best results, place the stem edge on the thick fold. Vary by using red, orange, yellow, and brown paper and mixing or overlapping strips of different colors. For spring, use shades of green.

thick fold

Pumpkins and Cats

Pumpkins

Cut from 4-inch-by-18-inch strips folded to be 4-inch-by-4½-inch rectangles. For variety, separately cut brown or green stems and glue them over the existing ones. Just for fun, use a black felt-tipped marking pen to transform some or all of the pumpkins into jack-o'-lanterns. Follow the pattern suggested here or create your own.

Black Cats

These cats won't bring bad luck if you pin, staple, or tack them securely to a bulletin board or wall. Cut them from 4-inch-by-18-inch strips folded to be 4-inch-by-4½-inch rectangles.

Ships and Turkeys

Ships

Ships under sail are reminiscent of the early explorers and settlers. Cut them from 4-inch-by-12-inch strips folded to be 4-inch-by-3-inch rectangles.

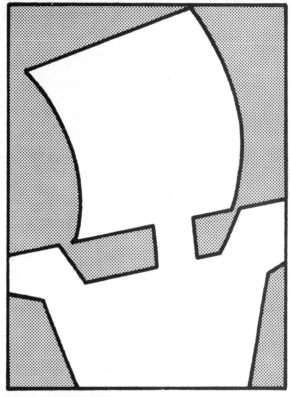

Turkeys

Thanksgiving wouldn't be complete without a turkey. Here's a whole flock of them to band or border your bulletin boards. Cut them from 3-inch-by-18-inch strips folded to be 3-inch-by-4½-inch rectangles.

Mice and Bells

Mice

For a December display, mice are nice. Cut them from 4-inch-by-12-inch strips folded to be 4-inch-by-3-inch rectangles. For best results, place the mouse's feet on the thick fold. Just for fun, use a felt-tipped marking pen to draw eyes and whiskers on some or all of your mice. Then glue on noses and ear linings cut from pink paper or felt. Follow the pattern provided here or create your own.

thick fold

Bells

Bells ring out the old year and ring in the new. Cut them from 3-inch-by-12-inch strips folded to be 3-inch-by-3-inch squares. For best results, place the top edge of the bell on the thick fold.

thick fold

Snowmen and Mittens

Snowmen

Welcome winter with a row of men made of snow. Cut them from 4½-inch-by-12-inch strips folded to be 4½-inch-by-3-inch rectangles. Just for fun, use a black felt-tipped marking pen to give some or all of your snowmen a black top hat, black eyes, a button nose, and a friendly smile.

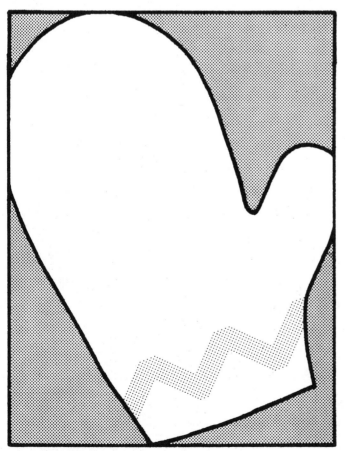

thick fold

Mittens

Keep out the winter cold with colorful mittens—not just a pair but a whole band or border of them. Cut them from 4½-inch-by-14-inch strips folded to be 4½-inch-by-3½-inch rectangles. For best results, position the pattern so that the thumb is at the thick fold. Just for fun, decorate the mittens with zigzags or other simple designs drawn or cut from paper of contrasting colors.

Hats and Hearts

Horizontal Hats

Commemorate Abraham Lincoln's birthday with a row of top hats. Cut them from 3½-inch-by-14-inch strips folded to be 3½-inch-by-3½-inch squares.

Vertical Hearts

Greet February with a bright border of hearts. Cut them from 4½-inch-by-16-inch strips folded to be 4½-inch-by-4-inch rectangles. For best results, place the top of the heart on the thick fold.

thick fold

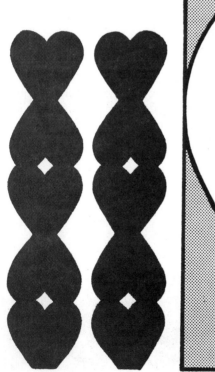

Shamrocks and Tulips

Shamrocks

Sure an' begorra, St. Patrick's Day is the time to wish for the luck o' the Irish and to wear a little green. Cut these shamrocks from 4-inch-by-18-inch strips folded to be 4-inch-by-4½-inch rectangles.

Tulips

March 20 or 21 is the Vernal Equinox, the first day of spring. Welcome this season with a border of pink, yellow, or red tulips. Cut them from 4-inch-by-18-inch strips folded to be 4-inch-by-4½-inch rectangles.

Umbrellas and Bunnies

Umbrellas

When April showers dampen your day, lift spirits with bands or borders of bright umbrellas. Cut them from 4-inch-by-16-inch strips folded to be 4-inch-by-4-inch squares.

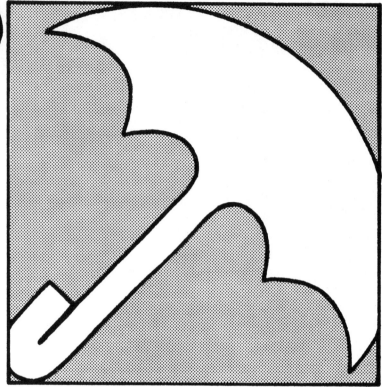

Bunches of Bunnies

For Easter or for spring, border a bulletin board with a bunch of bunnies. Cut them from 4½-inch-by-12-inch strips folded to be 4½-inch-by-3-inch rectangles. For variety, cut bunnies from paper in pastel colors rather than from white. Just for fun, use a felt-tipped marking pen to draw facial features on some or all of your bunnies. Follow the pattern provided here or create your own.

Daisies and Suns

Daisies

April showers bring May flowers. Freshen your room with dozens of daisies. Cut them from 4-inch-by-8-inch white strips folded to be 4-inch-by-2-inch rectangles. For best results, place the daisy center on the thick fold. After cutting, carefully unfold each two-daisy strip. As a variation, use a crayon or felt-tipped marking pen to add yellow centers or cut them from yellow construction paper and glue them in place.

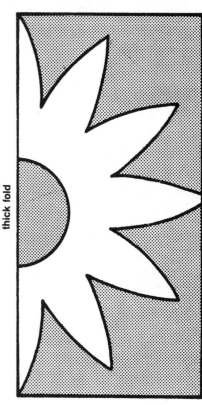

Suns

When May comes, the hot summer sun is not many days away. Cut these suns from yellow or orange 4-inch-by-16-inch strips folded to be 4-inch-by-4-inch squares and then folded once more to yield 4-inch-by-2-inch rectangles. For best results, place the center of the sun on the thick fold. As a variation, cut daisy shapes from orange paper and then pin, tack, staple, or glue them on yellow suns.

Answer Key

Page 86, The Book Clown
1. body
2. table of contents
3. glossary
4. bibliography
5. index

Page 88, Pickled Plurals
1. girls
2. benches
3. candies
4. boxes
5. leaves
6. men
7. cities
8. shoes
9. turkeys
10. windows

Page 89, Alphabet Animals
1. Andy
2. Boris
3. Carmen
4. Dexter
5. Homer
6. Manny
7. Travis
8. Zeke

Page 92, Spelling Riddle
Question: Where does a lamb go when it needs a haircut?
Answer: To the baa baa shop.

Page 106, Auntie Anteater's Addition
1. 5
2. 11
3. 12
4. 15
5. 9
6. 11
7. 12
8. 14
9. 15
10. 19
11. 17
12. 17
13. 31
14. 22
15. 32
16. 54

Page 107, Super Snake Subtraction
1. 5
2. 4
3. 7
4. 8
5. 6
6. 10
7. 14
8. 18
9. 11
10. 15
11. 24
12. 8

Page 108, Monster Math
1. $84
2. 37 marshmallows
3. 21 monsters
4. 9 gorbles
5. 32 scales

Page 111, Map Quiz
1. Alaska
2. Florida
3. Washington
4. Hawaii
5. Tennessee
6. six
7. Colorado
8. Kentucky
9. New Mexico
10. Nebraska

Page 113, North, South, East, or West?
1. east
2. west
3. west *and* east
4. north *and* south
5. west

Page 116, Who's in the Zoo?
1. A5
2. B4
3. E3 *and* F3
4. A3
5. C3
6. D2
7. D5
8. F1
9. E4
10. B1 *and* C1

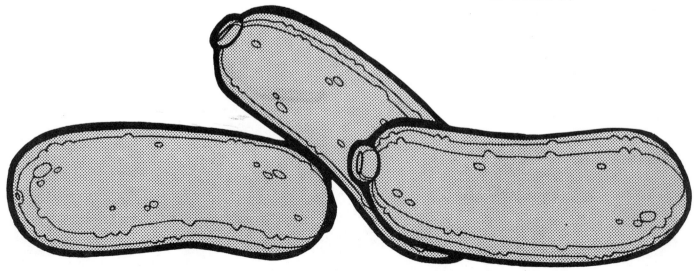